# RISK only money

## Success in Business Without Risking Family, Friends and Reputation

# Jack DeBoer

**Risk Only Money:**
Success In Business
Without Risking Family, Friends and Reputation
By Jack DeBoer

Edited by Diane McLendon
Cover Design by Worthington Martino
Designed by Amy Robertson

Published by Rockhill Books,
an imprint of Kansas City Star Books
1729 Grand Blvd.
Kansas City, Missouri 64108

First edition, first printing
Hardcover ISBN: 978-1-61169-010-1
Softcover ISBN: 978-1-61169-011-8
Library of Congress: 9781611690101

Printed in the United States.

www.RiskOnlyMoney.com

**ROCKHILL**
B O O K S

# What others are saying about Jack DeBoer

"When you are at the head of the rapids, fearful for what the journey through might bring, it is such a comfort to see someone who has already made it past the rough waters, smiling below the falls. This is Jack, sharing a life that reads as one great adventure, listening, learning from both success (and more often) failure, ultimately co-opting common sense while holding fast to the timeless values of honesty and the Golden Rule. I have known Jack and Marilyn for over 20 years. The truths spoken of in this book have been lived out in each of them. If we were only allowed two friends in life, we would be foolish not to claim the DeBoers!"

*—Ambassador Robert A. Seiple*
*Past President of World Vision;*
*CEO, Institute for Global Engagement*

---

"True greatness—true significance—is found in giving our lives to serve others, not in acquiring prestige, power, influence and money. In *Risk Only Money*, Jack DeBoer shares his own story of making it to the top, only to be taught some hard and humbling lessons when he got there. His story will challenge you to rethink your own definition of success. Are you willing to give of yourself? Your answer will say a lot about your future —and your own significance."

*—Richard Stearns*
*President of World Vision US*
*and author of* The Hole in Our Gospel

"*Risk Only Money* is a book rich in personal experiences. It reads like a novel but is factual in every respect. It is filled with lessons of success and failure and real lessons about honesty and integrity. While there are many references to the entrepreneur, the business observations are equally valid for corporate executives and the non-profit leader. You will be wiser after reading this book."

—*C. Fred Fetterolf*
*Retired President and Chief Operating Officer,*
*Aluminum Company of America*

---

"Jack's journey from the struggles, lessons and joys of success to the rewarding place of significance sets a high standard for others to emulate. His story is motivating and a good read."

—*Steve Reinemund*
*Retired Chairman and CEO PepsiCo;*
*Dean, The Schools of Business Wake Forest University*

---

"Jack believes in God's grace and that 'taking care of business' means honoring the Lord and sharing his blessings. In *Risk Only Money*, Jack offers a roadmap to others seeking fame and fortune. They may be surprised to find he takes them beyond material riches to a place of greater fulfillment. But they will be glad."

—*David Green*
*CEO and Founder, Hobby Lobby*

"Jack DeBoer painfully and candidly portrays his biggest business mistakes. In doing so, he helps the reader to determine if they are a manager or entrepreneur. For those entrepreneurs, he unlocks the golden nugget that long-term successful entrepreneurs don't work for money, but for a higher purpose, and in doing so they create a spiritual mission for themselves and those they lead."

*—Ed Flaherty*
*Entrepreneur and former owner of*
*Rapid Oil Change Company (sold to Valvoline Motor Oil)*
*and more than 100 hotels, shopping centers and Applebee's*
*restaurants; now a leader in the signage and display business*

---

"Business, like life, requires focused, motivated teamwork. Jack DeBoer would be the first to say that even the MVP couldn't win the game without full support, strategic risk—and a touch of magic."

*—Pat Williams*
*Senior VP and Co-Founder of the NBA'S Orlando Magic*

---

"You don't have to be in the lodging industry to find value in *Risk Only Money*. Anyone contemplating the road less traveled would be well served by studying Jack DeBoer's journey. He innovates rather than simply trotting out yesterday's answers for yesterday's travelers."

*—Horst Schultze*
*Chairman and CEO, West Paces Hotel Group*

❖

*Dedicated to the people*
*who helped me weather the storms*
*of business problems and to those*
*who will read this book*
*and find meaningful help*
*through the many lessons*
*I learned the hard way.*

❖

❖

*Thank you for your help and encouragement
in completing and marketing this book.*

*Fran and Fred Fetterolf*
*Sonia Greteman*
*Deanna Harms*
*Fritz King*
*Margaret Potter*
*Jonathan Rogers*
*Robert Tolley*

*—Jack DeBoer,*
*June 2011*

❖

# Table of Contents

# Prologue

# Risk Only Money...

For two days, I lay there in the darkness, shades drawn and the covers pulled over my head. I was paralyzed—with fear, with self-loathing, with shame, and with a realization that I didn't know what to do next.

I had hundreds of creditors I couldn't pay. Hundreds, affecting the lives of thousands of people. A few days before, one of them had called me on the phone. "I want my money by Friday or I'll kill you," he said.

"Who is this?" I asked.

"By Friday," he said. "Or you're a dead man." *Click.*

He hung up. I didn't know who to pay. I didn't know who to be afraid of. I only knew he was one of hundreds of people Jack P. DeBoer and Associates owed money to. He was one of the thousands of people I had hired—probably a contractor—to help realize my ego-fueled dreams of being America's biggest apartment builder.

How do you pay off hundreds and have an effect on the lives of thousands of people? There are plenty of towns in Kansas whose whole population is smaller than my creditor list. Where do you even begin? That phone call brought me face-to-face with the reality of my situation.

I tried to picture the man who had been on the other end of the phone. He was probably a contractor in some city where we were building yet another of the "Apartments that Jack Built"—another monument to me. I pictured the man pacing as he held the phone to his ear, his eyebrows knitted over slitted eyes, a vein bulging on his forehead, flecks of spittle flying as he yelled into the receiver.

And as I pictured that man—the man who had threatened my life—I saw him as a human being. I thought of the stress he must have been under because I hadn't paid him the money I owed him.

Maybe the man couldn't make payroll because of me. I knew what that was like; I had been there myself. But even payroll isn't just payroll. It's car payments, mortgage payments, electric bills, grocery bills, church tithes paid or skipped. It's children who get new shoes or continue to make do with the old ones. It's families who keep their houses or lose them.

Lying there in my bedroom, I realized that if that man, whoever he was, wanted to kill me, maybe he had good reason to do it.

Something about that realization changed everything for me. Up to that point, my business career had been all about me. My whole sense of self was wrapped up with businesses successes, with buildings and trucks with my name on them.

Less than one year earlier, I had turned down a $100 million offer for the business. Why? Because my main competitor had taken $100 million for his business. My goal in life had been to be the biggest apartment builder in America. Second-best wasn't good enough. Neither was a tie for first. My desire to be the person others looked up to because I was number one was so overblown that I turned down the $100 million rather than accept a tie for first place. In other words, business for me wasn't all about the money. I had been looking to business to give my life meaning and significance. I expected business success to earn me the love of my mother and my family, the respect of others, and even self-respect.

Now, on the brink of failure, I didn't know who Jack DeBoer was.

It was at that lowest moment—in the depths of failure, with my life in danger—that I made some realizations and commitments that would guide the rest of my career and life.

Lying there in bed, I stopped expecting business to do for me what business could never do. Business, I realized, was about one thing: making money. That sounds selfish, but stay with me. When I went into business, I incurred obligations to other people. Those people depended on me, just as they had people who depended on them. To meet my obligations, I would have to make money—and lots of it. But at this turning point I had finally found humility, and I was finished using money and success as a way to stand out in the minds of others.

In order to make sense of my situation, I put my business debts off to one side and thought long and hard about the rest of my life. I thought about what Jack DeBoer still had—not Jack DeBoer of Jack P. DeBoer and Associates, but Jack DeBoer the man. I focused on the things that had been a gift from God in how others were helping me in this time of need.

I zeroed in on eight non-monetary assets:

1. I still had my wife and family.
2. I still had my health.
3. I still had old friends who had stuck with me even if they thought my out-of-control ego was stupid.
4. I had not done anything illegal.
5. I still had plenty of energy.
6. I had always treated people with respect.

7. I had been truthful along the way.
8. I could now, finally, change who I was and how I would live my life going forward.

For all of my bad decisions, I hadn't lost those things. As I looked over my list, I understood something that has impacted every business decision I have made since. Doing business the wrong way could cause me to lose any or all of those eight assets—the most important assets I had. And yet those God-given gifts, if I lost them, could never be earned back by way of business. Money I could lose and earn back. But my family, reputation, self-respect, friendships, and health—those wouldn't be so easy to get back. They might even be impossible to get back. Those were things I couldn't afford to risk for any reason.

I made three big decisions before I climbed out of bed that day. The first was simply the decision to get out of bed. I was going to start chipping away at my debts and keep chipping until they were paid. Second, I decided to stop expecting business to do for me what business couldn't do. Business was good for one thing: making money. My third commitment grew out of the second. From that point on, in my business endeavors, I would risk only money. That's what money is for: risking, gaining, losing, gaining back and using it to help others in need. That was a risk I could live with. But I was finished risking everything else.

Before that personal crash, I rarely listened to the advice of others. That was a big part of my problem. When I got out of bed that day, I promised myself that if I managed to solve the problems I was facing, I would make every effort to help other people learn from my mistakes. To that end, I've made hundreds of speeches to businesses and student groups. This book is simply a continuation of that effort.

Part I:
**Striving**

# The Early Years

There is a pure, child-like entrepreneurial spirit that is free of ego—an enterprising nature that marvels at growth and industry for its own sake. It doesn't take long for self-serving, egotistical concerns to weasel their way in. But business in its purest form is all about investment, effort, and return. Pretty simple.

From my earliest years, I saw what it meant to struggle and claw to build a business from scratch. Before I was born, my Dutch-immigrant family had been comfortably middle class. My grandfather owned a lumberyard in Kalamazoo, Michigan, which was run by my father, Alfred DeBoer, and my father's brother-in-law.

But with the Great Crash of 1929—only a year and a half before I was born in January 1931—the lumberyard went under and my father found himself unemployed. He was a brilliant man, my father. He made all A's while earning a business degree from DePaul University in Chicago. He took the CPA exam on a bet and passed, though he never practiced as a CPA. But he unexpectedly found himself starting from scratch.

My mother, who had a degree in education from Western Michigan, took a series of government jobs and taught art in public schools while my father looked for a job. My parents ended up running a small real estate and insurance business; my father handled the real estate and my mother ran the insurance side. Money was tight, but we never really wanted for anything. My brother Paul, who is four years my senior, joined the Army after graduating from high school. I was what is now called a latchkey kid.

At ten years old, my business career began with pansies. Like many kids in the neighborhood in Kalamazoo, Michigan, I pulled a wagon to the pansy fields on Saturday mornings, bought a few flats of flowers, and rolled through the neighborhood reselling them.

It wasn't long, however, before I got a better idea. After building a three-level rack for the wagon and securing a very small loan from my father, I was the first boy at the pansy fields the next Saturday. I bought as many pansies as could fit on the wagon rack (at a volume discount, of course), and wheeled the tottering stack back to the neighborhood, where I sold the flats to my fellow pansy salesmen—the ones who didn't want to walk the two miles each way to the fields. My work was done by nine in the morning.

I had discovered wholesaling. I'm surprised it didn't occur to me to slap a Jack P. DeBoer and Associates logo on my delivery wagon. Soon enough, I would get into that kind of ego-stroking self-promotion. At that time, however, it was nice to be a businessman. It was a clean, uncomplicated thing. I bought pansies cheap then sold them for a little more than I bought them for. A willingness to get up a little earlier and walk a little farther than my peers turned a dollar into a dollar and a dime. Simple. Clean. Uncomplicated.

For a ten-year-old boy, it was a wondrous thing to see money grow like that. It seemed almost as miraculous as the little sprout that grew out of the butterbean I planted in a cup of soil for my science class. Forget about the me because that had nothing to do with it. It was sheer boyish wonder—a fascination with the alchemy that turned work and creativity into clinking silver in my pocket.

Soon it was time to start leveraging the assets. I saved my pansy money and bought a power mower—the old kind with a reel and a motor on top. I was going into the lawn mowing business.

There was just one problem—one I'm now surprised that I hadn't foreseen. My first business setback came in the form of swollen, watery eyes and angry red hives up and down my arms. I was allergic to grass.

The entrepreneurial mind is an optimistic mind—often to an unrealistic degree. It is hard to see the downside or the limitations on the front end of an opportunity. A grass allergy is a pretty serious limitation for a person who has set himself up as a lawn care specialist. I was looking at the potential dollar signs, not the possible limitations. Such unrealistic optimism can obviously be a serious problem; we have to train ourselves to count the costs, challenges, and potential downsides, realistically. That's not to say that it's wise to avoid all risk, only that we ought to be realistic about the risks we take.

I've been a part of many business start-ups. Some succeeded; most failed. By "failed," I simply mean they didn't make money. In some cases, I took calculated risks that just didn't work out. There's no shame in that. Other times, I failed to recognize downside potential. I don't suppose there's real shame in that either, as long as you learn from your mistakes, accept the blame, and are willing to dust yourself off and start over again.

I think it's probably a good thing that entrepreneurs are by nature overly optimistic going into a venture. Otherwise we might never pull the trigger. "Ready, Aim, Fire?" I was more likely to say, "Ready, Fire, Aim." I expected to have to readjust after things got rolling.

My grass allergy didn't spell the end of the mowing business. The business problem, I soon learned, was a business opportunity. I started renting out the mower to other enterprising boys—and let them do the mowing. At ten years old, I already understood that others working for me was the way to go.

Working for myself meant being willing to work hard—no shirking, no half-stepping. Being an entrepreneur means working 16 hours for you in order to avoid working eight hours for somebody else.

As a boy I did a lot of things to make money. I shoveled snow, washed cars, sold magazines to the staff at Kalamazoo State Hospital. My parents had taught me how to save and reinvest. When my friends were blowing whatever money they had on milkshakes and entertainment and old jalopies, I was saving and reinvesting.

I got my driver's license when I turned 14. That same day, my dad sent me on an errand to Grand Rapids in his 1941 Plymouth. I drove the 50 miles alone—the day I got my license! But that's the kind of dad I had. He was always willing to hand over responsibility that would stretch my brother and me. He knew we would rise to the occasion. It's a confidence I've benefited from all my life—both self-confidence and a confidence in those who work with and for me.

At 17, I had my Michigan real estate license. I helped my father in my parents' real estate and insurance business, called Property and Insurance Exchange. I never had much to do with Dad's other business: He had a following of people for whom he filed their taxes. I remember him coming home with dollar bills sticking out of his pockets—pay for completing others' tax returns.

We weren't part of the board of realtors. Most of our business was in very low-priced houses, and most sales were financed by land contracts that my dad sold to a group of retired investors. It was a pretty hard way to make a living. Life for my parents was work, work, and more work. Their social circle consisted of six or eight friends and relatives. The only time I ever went to the country club was as a caddy.

Through hard work and determination, my folks pulled themselves up from having lost everything to a good life with a cottage at West Lake (it cost $1,500) and a new car every couple of years. Every Christmas they took us to Key West, Florida—the only time they took off the whole year. They had lost their house in the Depression, but just as I was starting college, they built a new one just a block away from the first one. It took 17 long, hard years, but they were back.

Life was very satisfying and straightforward back then. We lived in a black and white world where right was right and wrong was wrong. We always knew the rules. There was no gray area, no pretending that the rules didn't exist or didn't matter. That's not to say we always followed them, but at least we knew it when we were in the wrong. My path was clear: I was to find a good woman, get married, and work to support a family. That is one thing I got right. But I have to confess that getting it right had more to do with the luck of finding the right woman than it had to do with my efforts. Yes, luck in that Marilyn, when she was a senior at Central High School, put an ad in the paper looking for a part-time secretarial job. My father hired her sight unseen and over the phone.

I'll never forget the first house I sold—a small house on a corner in Kalamazoo. It sold for $4,500 with $250 down. Like most of the houses sold through Property and Insurance Exchange, it was financed through a land contract. The buyers borrowed the down payment from a small loan company. I thought I was a real estate genius—a real tycoon. My share of the commission, after all, was almost $100! If I had really been a genius, I would have bought the place instead of selling it. That corner is now home to a McDonald's.

Even when I was a second-year student at Michigan State, I was still riding a bicycle. My mother told me I could buy a car on two conditions: It had to be a new car, and I had to pay cash for it. From a very young age, my folks had taught me how to use a ledger to keep track of every penny I earned and spent. I watched my balance until I had saved enough money to buy a new car. It was a 1950 Chevrolet. The price: $1,700.

Not much later, the Korean War broke out. We were only five years beyond World War II, so rationing was still fresh in people's minds. They were afraid that new cars would once again be unavailable, just as they had been during World War II. The demand for late-model used cars spiked. I had a nearly new car and an eye for opportunity. Just a few months after buying that Chevy, I sold it for a tidy profit.

I was proud of my transaction. I had made money; wasn't that what business transactions were all about? But my mother cried. For my mother, the purchase of that car—and its sale—was about much more than money. There was a whole emotional component that I was still a little too naïve (or maybe too wise) to grasp. For my mother, that car was a symbol of my success. Actually, I suppose it was a symbol of her success too. She and my father had raised the kind of boy who could work hard, save his money, and buy himself a new car for cash. She was proud of me, and she hated to see that car go away.

I didn't quite understand what my mother was crying about. But I filed that episode away nevertheless: Making money and buying things didn't just make me feel better about my situation, it made my mother proud. When I accomplished good things in my business affairs, I felt that my mother loved me, even though she never told me she did. How much would I have to accomplish, I wondered, in order to hear her say those words I so cherished, though I had never heard them from her: "I love you."

It wouldn't be completely honest to suggest that ego wasn't part of what drove me in those earliest years of my "career."

The early success I enjoyed definitely built up my sense of self. I liked the accolades I got from people who were impressed by what seemed to be a Midas touch. Everybody knows that a car is supposed to depreciate the minute you drive it off the sales lot, but I sold my new car for a profit. And what lawn-mowing "professional" finds out he's allergic to grass *after* he invests in and starts a lawn-mowing business ... and still comes out ahead?

In those early years, I gained quite a bit of confidence in my instincts, problem-solving abilities, common sense, and even luck. It is a confidence that has served me well—except when it has gotten me in trouble. In later chapters, we will see how much of this success and satisfaction has real value—and how much it's just an inflated sense of who you are.

But confidence isn't the same thing as ego. Sure, there was self-praise in the young Jack DeBoer, but it wasn't yet the driving force of my life. In my case, these successes meant using the business (or the person or situation) to build up my own sense of who I was. This kind of thinking always gets in the way of what business is really about—which is making money. That's counterintuitive. You would think that moneymaking and ego would go hand in hand. But they don't have to. And they shouldn't. If your reason for making money is to feed your inflated sense of who you are and to impress others, you can't be a really effective businessperson. Your business decisions will be driven by the wrong motivations. You may hold it together for a while, but it's going to come crashing down eventually. You have to make business decisions based on what's good for the business—not based on what you think is going to be good for you.

At that point in my life, one reason I was still able to make business decisions based on the hard facts of profit and loss— that is to say, I was able to risk only money—was because the material things I wanted didn't outstrip the amount of money I was able to make. That 1950 Chevrolet was a fine car, and I was mighty proud of it. But I wasn't so proud of it that I missed the chance to sell it for a profit. In other words, in that instance, my concern of how others perceived me didn't stand in the way of my business sense. It wasn't many years later before the "me first" in my decision-making would cost me dearly—$95 million, to be precise.

I was entrepreneurial from Day One. From my pansy-selling days on, I always worked for myself. I was never an employee—except for one brief stint as a soda jerk. I went away to Michigan State and took a job at a soda shop in the dorm where I was living. I wanted to be the best soda jerk in the world. One night I was putting on a show for the customers, demonstrating my ability to run five Hamilton Beach blenders at one time. As I got the fifth one going, I didn't realize that I hadn't put it quite into place. I turned to face the counter, quite satisfied with myself, and the canister spun off the machine and into the next canister, which flung into the next canister, which spun into the next and into the next. Malted milk and ice cream spun in every direction, spattering everybody on either side of the counter—including my boss, the 60-year-old woman who ran the place. Her next words to me turned out to be her last: "You're fired!" My first and last job was over and I never worked for anyone again.

I guess you could say that I was an employee of the Army during the Korean War. But at the time, I didn't really think of myself as an employee so much as Eisenhower's partner in running the world. Small successes were transforming this humble entrepreneur. The successes were feeding a complete personality change. Doing business was starting to have a dark, new meaning for me.

# Self-Assessment

Maybe this is a good time to ask yourself exactly why you're in business, or why you want to be.

1. Are you trying to earn love?
2. Are you just keeping score?
3. Do you only want expensive toys, a yacht and a jet airplane?
4. Are you trying to avoid having a boss?
5. Do you hope to achieve status?
6. Are you in it for the money?
7. Are you trying to impress someone or people?

If you answered "yes" to any of these besides #6, let me suggest that you reassess your approach to business. Business is about making money, providing jobs, and driving the basics of the American dream. If you have other expectations about what business is going to do for you as a person, you're going to be disappointed. Save your emotional energy for other parts of your life—family, friends, community involvement. The money you make by tending to your business (and keeping your business in perspective) will fuel those other aspects of your life.

The American system allows success and failure, losing and regaining money. If you make every business decision with money as the central theme and surround the decision with all the other important things that are outlined in this book, your decision process will be most healthy and effective. You'll build a foundation that will serve you well through ups and downs as you turn failure into success.

# The Perils of Procrastination

Are you a procrastinator? If so, you'd better get a job. You won't make it as a businessperson. If you're a procrastinator in your personal life, you'd better fix it if you're going to be an entrepreneur. In business, good things *don't* come to those who wait. If you procrastinate in business, you've probably already achieved your highest level. If you're happy there, good for you. But if you want to continue to grow, you can't procrastinate.

Define what's important to you, and then get after it. And don't just *look* busy. Busy-ness doesn't really matter in business. What matters is that you know your task and then do the task. If you don't quite know your task and yet you're still busy, you're looking at the worst of both worlds. You're probably doing a lot of unimportant things. If you don't have time to yourself, you aren't planning your success. If you're answering more calls than you're placing, you're not running your life, somebody else is. Success in business is all about being in charge of as much as you can be in charge of or responsible for … and not waiting to see what's going to happen next.

We only have so much brain space. When we procrastinate, we fill our minds with "oh, I have to's" or "oh, I should have's." There's no space for what is important if our brains are filled with this kind of thinking. Every day, I do something about everything I can do something about. I return every call before the day ends, to cleanse the brain. Voicemail is your friend.

We have all watched Charlie Rose interview successful people from all walks of life. Five nights a week for more than 20 years he has interviewed super achievers.

The other night I heard him say, "Of all the hundreds of interviews I have done, never one time did a guest say that they felt their success was a result of being smarter, better looking or more charming. Each said it came from having a passion for what they were doing and working hard to achieve the defined goals of their dreams."

# Two Rules for the Salesperson (That Means You)

The starter for the engine of business is sales. In a certain sense, we're all salespeople. I haven't sold a lot of "products" since I got out of the pansy business, but I sell ideas to bankers when I'm raising money for projects. I sell my companies' reputation when we make deals with franchisees or vendors or when I'm looking to hire. I sell to cities that have to understand our concept before they approve developments we want to build. Business is sales, sales, sales, and not just for the "salespeople."

All of us who sell (in other words, all of us in business) need to understand a few important rules:

**1. Getting to "no" is as important as getting to "yes."** We all want to get a "yes" from the person we're selling to. But sometimes wishful thinking results in wasted time and effort in pursuit of a sale that's never going to happen. The really good salesperson is good at understanding the situation. And sometimes that means quickly getting to "no" and moving on to somebody who's going to say "yes." Wishful thinkers do not belong in sales.

**2. Celebrate when the deal is totally done.** I know sales folks who celebrate when they think the sale has a good chance of being made, then celebrate when the contract is signed, then finally celebrate again when the deal is closed. Save your celebrating until after the money changes hands and you get your commission in the bank. Don't talk about having sold something until the deal is actually done.

**3. Know when to shut up.** I need to say something to actual salespeople: Once the contract is signed, shut up and stop selling. Sales types who keep selling after the deal is signed always seem to make matters worse. I have never met a really good sales person who was good at the follow-up details that are better left to other people in the company.

One last comment on sales: When a business is struggling, most businesspeople assume the solution must be more sales or more volume. Your first reaction really should be to see if you can carefully cut costs without impacting the top line. Costs are something you have some control over. Sales, on the other hand, depend on variables that are often beyond your control. Just remember, if there's any way you can avoid it, don't make cost cuts that will make it impossible to keep, protect, or grow the top line. Those are the kind of cuts that might happen when it's time to shut the business down.

# 2

# Life in Uniform

s you develop your own leadership style, one of the first questions you need to ask yourself is, "Am I a manager or an entrepreneur?" An entrepreneur is a person who pursues opportunities beyond his or her resources. An entrepreneur also tends to miscalculate the risks. An entrepreneur looks out at the horizon and says, "I want to go there," starts in that direction, and then wonders how to get the resources to get there. A manager, on the other hand, is a person who looks at the existing resources and says, "How do we maximize these resources to get us toward where we want or need to be?" Every business needs both entrepreneurial minds and managerial minds, and generally the entrepreneur is the boss who knows how important it is to listen to the manager. Know which one you are. And know that you aren't both. Know your weaknesses. And surround yourself with people who complement you with their strengths. I first learned this lesson in the Army.

I went through the ROTC program at Michigan State. All of my life I had wanted to fly airplanes, so after the two basic years in ROTC, I applied for advanced Air Force ROTC. I flunked the physical for the Air Force because I have hammertoes—toes that are permanently bent. To this day I still don't know how bent toes interfere with flying an airplane. But I wasn't fated to join the flyboys. Instead, I decided to join my roommate and mentor Bob Girardin in Military Police ROTC. He introduced me to Colonel Theiring, who got me into the program.

My feet weren't good enough for the Air Force, so I ended up in the infantry. Yeah, it doesn't make much sense to me either. In any case, I loved ROTC and the formality and structure of the military. I excelled and became the second-highest ranked cadet at Michigan State. I met General Douglas McArthur and spent time at West Point. It was a great, all-around experience.

After graduating from Michigan State, I went into the Army as a Second Lieutenant stationed at Fort Bragg, North Carolina. We were in the middle of the Korean War, but since I was bulletproof (aren't all young men in their early 20's bulletproof?), I didn't worry too much about my safety. I gave more thought to my impending wedding. I was going to marry Marilyn Sanders, my high school sweetheart, on September 12th, 1953.

But then in August 1953, about one month before our wedding date, I received orders to report to Far East Command (Korea). I wasn't the least bit concerned about getting hurt. I just didn't know how I was going to tell Marilyn that I was to report and be shipped out two days before our wedding date.

I was walking around, thinking it over, when I saw my Battalion Supply Officer and my Commanding Officer, Colonel Stratton, coming from the other direction. As we passed, the supply officer said to the Colonel, "What do you think about DeBoer going to Korea?" The Colonel looked me in the eye, and something he saw there betrayed what was happening inside of me. Keep in mind I was a clean-boots, spit-and-polish, tall-standing, working-harder-than-most type and the colonel's favorite.

"You don't want to go, do you, DeBoer?" he asked.

"Well, Sir," I said, "I'd be more than happy to go—it's not about Korea. It's just that I'm trying to figure out what to tell my fiancée. I'm supposed to report for duty on September 10th. Well, you see, I'm scheduled to report to the altar on September 12th."

The Colonel motioned for me to follow him to his office. There he called a Colonel Campbell in Washington. The next day, my orders were changed. When my BOQ (Bachelor Officers Quarters) roommate, Bill Jordan, heard about my orders, he said, "I wish I knew what my orders were!" Jordan wanted to go into politics and thought a stint in Korea would help him; people like voting for veterans, after all.

The next day, Jordan did have those orders for himself. I don't know how he swung it. I was stunned; I didn't like the idea of my roommate going to Korea in my place. I told him, "If you go over there and get yourself killed, I'll never forgive you!" The thought of Bill Jordan getting hurt haunted me every day until he returned safely.

So Marilyn and I got married as planned and went on with our life at Fort Bragg in Fayetteville, North Carolina, while Jordan went off to Korea. Marilyn got a job at the post hospital, and I carried on with my duties as a military police officer.

There was always something interesting going on at work. A new commander came on board for the 82nd Airborne, and we soon found out that he was a real stickler when it came to traffic. "Accidents don't just happen," he was fond of saying, "they're caused." In other words, he wanted to be sure somebody got a ticket any time there was a traffic mishap on the base, no matter how small.

One day, when I was the post duty military police officer, we got a call that there had been an accident on Bragg Boulevard—a rainy day, a school bus, an Oldsmobile. The duty sergeant and I headed over to see what had happened. The Oldsmobile looked familiar—same model and color as the one my parents had just helped us buy as a wedding present. And the woman standing in the rain talking to the bus driver looked familiar too: Marilyn. It didn't take any time to realize who was at fault in the accident—my new wife.

Nobody was hurt, and though our Oldsmobile was pretty smashed up, there was no damage whatsoever to the bus. The duty sergeant looked like he was trying to suppress a grin. "You know what the commander says," I said to the sergeant. "Accidents don't just happen."

"Yeah?" he said.

"Well, I think maybe this one just happened."

The sergeant smiled at me and then at Marilyn. "It's a rainy day," he said. "These things happen."

A couple of hospital paychecks later, the Oldsmobile was as good as new.

---

But I should back up to a day earlier in the summer before we married. I was in the orderly room of Battalion Headquarters when everyone heard the Battalion Commander shout out an expletive and storm out of his office. As he went past me he said, "DeBoer, you are now Company Commander of D Company!" And out the door he went. Everyone in the office was shocked, but nobody was more shocked than I was. A Second Lieutenant as Company Commander?

As inconspicuously as I could, I walked out of the office and headed for the officers' quarters to avoid having to face anyone. I spent an hour in my room, hoping that the commander would calm down and the crisis would pass. Thinking it was safe to return, I headed back to the Company office. When I walked in the room, all the enlisted personnel stood up. That was new; they had never done that for me before.

I looked around the room like a deer in the headlights. Then I remembered some advice my older brother had given me when he pinned on my bars at my commissioning ceremony. He had gone into the military as an enlisted man a few years before I did. "Remember," he said, "if you want to stay out of trouble in the military, earn the confidence of a Master Sergeant and you will be just fine."

Across the way I saw Sergeant Huey, the top-ranking enlisted man in the Company. "Huey, we need to talk," I said.

"All right," he said.

"Let's go where we can sit down," I said.

"Why not your office?" said Huey. I gave him a confused look. I didn't have an office. Sergeant Huey gestured toward the Company Commander's office.

"Oh, yeah," I said. "My office."

I wasn't quite ready to sit behind the desk, so Sergeant Huey and I sat across from each other in two hard-backed metal chairs in front of the desk. We sat there and looked at each other for what seemed like an hour. Then I made one of the best decisions of my life.

"Huey," I said, "I don't know anything about running a company. But you're a 25-year veteran. So why don't we make a deal. I'll wear the bars. I'll catch the salutes. You'll run Company D. And I'll listen more than I talk."

A grin spread across Huey's face. "Lieutenant," he said, "you and I are going to get along just fine."

From that moment on, Company D was the best at absolutely everything. We won every competition we entered at Fort Bragg. We got complimentary letters from the commanding General of the 18th Airborne.

That was a great management lesson for me, and one I've never forgotten. Thankfully, I had sense enough to know that I was an entrepreneur, not a manager. There were plenty of things I thought I was good at, but running Company D wouldn't have been one of them. The lesson I learned seems obvious, but it's surprising how many people never learn it. It's simply this: Pick the best horse, and give it its head.

First, you have to take your time making sure you've got the right people working for you. Then, give those people the freedom to do what they think is best. I had seen enough of Sergeant Huey to know that he was the man most qualified to run Company D. He had been in the Army longer than I had been on Earth!

But my best move wasn't putting Huey in charge; it was staying out of his way. I let him do exactly what I had "hired" him to do. Huey soon learned that asking my forgiveness was better than asking my permission. I gave him the freedom to be his best, and he made our organization the best.

There have been times when I have failed to take my own advice—I have dabbled in micro-management every now and again. But usually, once I have hired them, I have had sense enough to stay out of my employees' ways.

---

What happens when a manager can't tell the difference between being thought of as a tough boss and an effective boss? Disaster—that's what happens. I've hired several managers who have made that mistake. A senior officer at one of our hotel chains was solicitous and charming towards his boss. But when he related to his subordinates, the charm went away; he was tough, unyielding, uninterested, aloof, and demanding. None of those qualities have anything to do with effective leadership. None of those traits result in better performance by subordinates. He should have been cultivating descriptors like consistent, interested, truthful, dependable, complimentary, helpful and caring, and combining that with clear expectations of his subordinates.

Being in a position of power doesn't always mean you have to use that power. When possible, an effective leader does not look for situations in which he can be tough, unyielding or demanding. That's the worst kind of ego trip. An effective leader saves that sort of thing for when he really needs it. If everyone around you knows you have power, you don't have to use it very often.

It truly is amazing what a manager can accomplish when he doesn't care who gets the credit—and when he's willing to accept blame for his mistakes, and even, to a certain degree, the mistakes of people under his leadership.

For awhile, one of our yachts was captained by a man who was never wrong—or, rather, never admitted that he was wrong. When it came to operating the vessel, he was extremely competent. Bill was professional, entertaining, and charming. But he never admitted to being in the wrong about anything. I suppose that would be a tenable position for a person who is actually perfect. But I don't know anybody who's perfect.

In this guy's case, it wasn't just that he was never wrong, it was also that he didn't want to give anybody else credit for being right. He treated the crew's successes as if they were his, but anything that went wrong on the boat, well that went back on the crew's side of the ledger. And he was always telling his boss (me) about their shortcomings, both real and imagined. He blamed little things on the crew as if he was preparing me for bigger problems to come—which he also blamed on the crew. He made snide comments about crewmembers' sexual orientations, spending habits, and relationships with fellow workers. He said the stewardesses were likely to quit and that any training was wasted on them. He said the first mate had a bad personality—something that I never noticed myself. He said the chef spent too much money on food. It was always something.

I believe that any time Marilyn or I praised or showed any kindness to a crewmember, that was the beginning of the end for that person. The captain had it in for them from that moment on. In time, little lies came to light, and it became clear how damaging his behavior had been. Bear in mind, a boat crew is a very tight team. They work together 24/7. They live in close quarters. The job requires close coordination. In such an intense work environment, the captain's damaging remarks were ten times more damaging than those of a boss in a different setting.

I was slow to see the signs, but here's my advice to you: If you've hired a manager who always wants to talk about the failures of his staff, I can almost guarantee you it's not the staff you need to worry about. It's the manager. By the time I got rid of that captain, our boat had come to be known as a revolving door. We lost a lot of good crew members who were smart enough to refuse to work in such an environment.

So, what is the lesson? If you want to advance in life and business, hire people who are better than you and give credit where credit is due. Let your boss know how great the people who work for you are and take your share of the blame, plus a little extra. I love what President Truman said: "The buck stops here." Are you the kind of leader who is actually willing to take that kind of responsibility? If you are, you'll find that the people you're responsible for will begin to take their responsibilities seriously too.

My dad always said that the world would be a better place if everyone were one job lower. People tend to get promoted up to the level where they're often incompetent. Unfortunately, they often deal with that incompetence and self-doubt by pretending to be more competent than they are, or, what's worse, pretending that the people around them are incompetent so they don't have to face their own issues.

The best managers I have ever worked with have a common trait. I call it ego control with self-confidence. I'm not saying you shouldn't have any ego. If you are going to work hard, which is what it takes to get ahead, you need to have controlled self worth along with all the other traits and skills that leaders have—communication skills, the ability to motivate, organization, adaptability, etc. But there's a big difference between ego and those traits. You can't have too much skill at communicating, be too organized, too interested in other people, or too healthy. You can't be too good as a planner, too good at relationships, or too open-minded (actually, perhaps you *can* sometimes be too open-minded). Be as good a planner as you can be; the sky's the limit for resourcefulness and willingness to listen.

But ego—that's the one that you need just a little of. You need just enough to make you take pride in your work and care about your reputation. A little dab will do you. Trust me. I'm an expert in that department. Don't lose your pride, just control it. Remember, you're not in business to build yourself, but to build the business. You're in business to make money. I know from experience that any ego stroking you might get from business affects your decisions and is most often short-lived. Focus on making money, then let your self worth follow. Or to put it in leadership terms, if you pay attention to building up your team members instead of your own little empire, you'll find that business offers up a whole new kind of pride and satisfaction that you would never get if pride and satisfaction were your primary goal.

---

But I've gotten ahead of myself. We were in Fort Bragg, and my personal combat with why I was in business hadn't started yet. Those years in Fort Bragg were good years. My new wife, Marilyn, and I lived off base in a small rental house in Fayetteville. Our friends were mostly newly married couples; we all made the same amount of money and had the same interests. My only worry in those days was Bill Jordan, the old roommate who had gone to Korea in my place. And he came out just fine. He served his tour, returned safely home, became an FBI agent, and lived happily ever after. Thank God.

However, it was during that time that a dark cloud began to form on the horizon. My reasons for dreaming of my own business were getting distorted. I had my own office. I had my own driver—who was also a college-educated man. My personal Jeep had a sign on the spare tire cover: Company Commander, 503<sup>rd</sup> Military Police Battalion, Company D. I had the shiniest shoes on the base, and the men saluted when I walked past.

It seems ironic, but it was during that period when I wasn't making much money that my self-pride problem really began to take shape. I suppose it was because my stint in the Army was the first time my work ever began to fill certain voids that I had felt all my life. I had never been part of the "in" crowd in school—I was always on the outside socially. That began to change when I joined the Theta Chi fraternity at Michigan State. I felt accepted, part of a brotherhood. It was a real life changer for sure.

But it was in the military that I really started to feel that I had the respect of other people, and I liked it. I was an officer and a leader. I felt like I was somebody—a force to be reckoned with. A lot of good things happened to me during my years in the military. But with them came an addiction that would threaten to consume all. I am not talking about drugs or alcohol. I am talking about the new era of self-importance. As I think back, I am not sure I would have really liked me much.

# The Blame Game

How many people do you know who never take any blame? If you're always blaming other people, eventually you're going to get your head handed to you. A liar knows when he's lying. A chronic blamer, on the other hand, doesn't have as much self-awareness as a chronic liar. A blamer begins to believe he's never wrong. He ends up twisting the truth to fit his version of things— the version in which things are never his fault. And before long, he falls into a trap and isn't aware he's lying.

Once you get used to blaming other people, blame just rolls off of your tongue in every minor incident. It creates a completely toxic work environment. When you hear someone constantly blaming others, watch out: It's only a matter of time before you're the target of his blame game.

If you recognize the blame habit in yourself, be thankful that you were able to see it. Maybe you're not too far-gone. Set about fixing the problem. The best way is to get in the habit of taking more blame than you really think is yours to take. I think you'll find that the rewards of taking blame are greater than the rewards of passing the blame to someone else. I know, it sounds backwards, but just try it. Once you've accepted blame, you've taken all of the tension out of a potentially explosive situation. Your reputation goes up, not down, when you accept blame and do something about it. A person who is willing to accept blame is a person who can be trusted. We all do stuff that doesn't go the way we planned—big things and little things. Every-

*(continued)*

body understands that. They're surprisingly willing to forgive once you quit trying to cover your own behind.

When I think back over the tough times in my business life, one of the most important strengths I had that helped me recover was the fact that I blamed myself for my problems, not others. With very few exceptions, people said, "So, okay, you screwed up. Now let's get on with life."

# The Question I Always Ask a Job Reference

**Hiring the right people is vital. You better do it well.**

Modern employment law has made it tricky to get any useful information out of a job applicant's references. It seems that a former employer does not want to give you the straight dope when it comes to a less-than-stellar employee. If their answers cost a person a job, there's always the possibility that they could get sued. And even if the chances of losing such a lawsuit are slim for the former employer, it's not really worth the trouble or the risk. So you have to learn to read between the lines.

If you ask, "Is this person totally trustworthy in your opinion and experience?" there's a 95 percent chance that the reference is going to say, "Yes." That's not what I'm listening for. I'm listening for any hesitation on the part of the former employer. Anything short of "Oh, absolutely!" or "I trust her completely!" is a signal. Another tip is to ask questions about a former employee's performance rather than about his character. There are fewer laws restricting the answers a reference can give you about an employee's *performance.*

I have a standard question that I always ask: " If you needed the skills of this employee, would you rehire this person?" It's a simple yes-or-no question that gives the reference the chance to tell the truth without violating any laws.

# 3

# As Luck Would Have It

*n this country, if you get a good education, work hard, think creatively, and are honest in your dealings and your life, you can expect a solid, middle-class existence. The real difference between a solid, middle-class existence and great wealth is largely luck. One key to successful business is simply being able to survive until you get lucky. Even the smartest of businessmen will get hammered by forces outside of their control. One hundred dollar a barrel oil makes many in the oil business look very smart, but $10 oil, well that is a different story. Sometimes it is true that we would all rather be lucky than be smart.*

I would have made the Army a career, but I realized that, up through Major, everyone would be promoted based not on merit, but on time spent in grade. That took away a lot of incentive to work harder to get ahead. It wasn't an environment where I wanted to make a career. So when my time was up, we went home.

Marilyn and I returned to Kalamazoo and moved into my parents' cottage at West Lake—that basic place they had bought for $1,500. I joined my father's real estate and insurance business and started my career. Marilyn and I were starting from scratch. We literally had no savings; we made less than $200 a month in the Army. All we had was a free and clear car. But we were ready to take on the world.

I wanted to grow the business, so we came up with a slogan: "We sell a house every 24 hours." It was a slogan well before it was a reality. And in Kalamazoo, Michigan, in 1954 (population 70,000 or so), making that claim a reality was no small task. But we did it, and with a sales force of just five. The average price of the homes we sold was less than $10,000. In the first new subdivision we worked in, the houses sold for $6,950. Payments on those houses, including taxes and insurance, were about $40 a month! Our first source of financing was under the GI Bill: Veterans could buy with no money down, or FHA with very little money down. We sold some of those houses on land contracts; in other words, some buyers couldn't secure VA, FHA, or conventional financing, so Property and Insurance Exchange, or investors my father found, held the deed and the buyers made monthly payments to us rather than to the bank or savings and loan. The idea was for the buyer to eventually get into a position where he could get a conventional mortgage, at which point we or our investors stepped out from the middle of the deal. My dad loved poor people, and he got a lot of satisfaction out of helping them get into houses.

That "every 24 hours" claim made us get creative in a market where a lot of buyers couldn't even come up with a small down payment. I made many trips to Detroit, where the VA offices were located, and Grand Rapids, where FHA was located, to convince them to approve our buyers. In those days, the wife's income, if she had any, wasn't counted in the loan qualification unless she could produce a note from a doctor saying that she couldn't get pregnant. These days it's hard to imagine, but that was the way it was. We often arranged for the buyers to get loans from non-bank lenders who made loans up to $500. The small loan companies liked this business and, of course, we liked it too.

But the small-loan scenario wasn't ideal—or, in any case, it wasn't for everybody. Those were relatively high-interest loans. In those days, banks had what they called Christmas clubs. If you were in the Christmas club, throughout the year you put a little money into an account each week that you had earmarked for Christmas. The bank paid no interest on these accounts. Then, when December rolled around, you took your money out of the account to pay for Christmas gifts. Stores had lay-away programs that let people pay a little at a time for the things they wanted or needed. Of course, they did not get the goods until they were paid for; rather than buying on credit, they bought on patience.

I thought, "Why not do a Christmas club for our customers?" So we introduced the "Lay-Away-a-Home" program. First-time buyers put away a few dollars each month toward a down payment. And it worked. We had a nice pipeline of people who had saved between $300 and $500 for a down payment that would put them into home ownership.

One thing I know now that I didn't know then: You get the most appreciation in the most expensive properties. I have often thought that if I were to start over again in the real estate business, I would put together a group of investors and buy the highest-priced, best property I could find in new, upscale developments. Anybody who did that over the last 20 years made piles of money on each of those properties—recession or no recession. Well, at least until 2008 when the entire economic world changed—nothing is forever. In our current business, my instructions are to go upscale or go downscale, but stay out of the middle-priced world. The mid-range is a commodity; it rises and falls with forces over which you have no control. Unfortunately, the financial world has engineered the equity out of our middle class and recovery will take years.

It is astounding to think about what has happened to the single-family house business and financing during my career. In the old days, a starter home was less than 800 square feet with one bath. These days, a starter home is more likely to approach 1,700 square feet with a two-car garage and two and a half baths. The difference? Wives went to work and creative financing became available so families could pay for bigger houses. Even the kids have helped pay for these bigger houses—by becoming latchkey kids. I strongly believe that those bigger homes were the beginning of a total social change for families in this country.

The really unfortunate change has been the financial engineering of Wall Street and others to steal the home equity from American families by allowing 100 percent-plus loans, second mortgages, and easy approval for new loans. The second mortgages made money available to pay off credit cards, but took away equity for the future. That was fine as long as home values were going up every year, but when home values started to go down—well, from 2008 on, we've all seen what that led to.

---

In a place like Kalamazoo, Michigan, you can't sell a house every 24 hours without significantly adding to the inventory. In the late 1950's, we developed Southland Village—100 acres on the south side of the city. The family that owned the property was scattered across the country, and since I did not have any money, I had to convince each of the family members to sell the land to me and take their money as I was able to develop it.

I had to go to five cities. My mother went with me, flying in the prop-driven airliners of the time. I was successful in getting all of the family members to sign on and sold off the commercial land to raise money for the residential portion of the land. Not bad for a 26-year-old kid. I hoped my mother was proud of me. But even as she traveled with me and saw me do what, I at least thought, I was really good at, it was hard to know for sure.

In Southland Village, we built 100 or more houses in the $15,000 to $40,000 range. Getting houses finished on our breakneck schedule was a huge challenge. We put up signs that said, "WE WORK ON EVERY HOUSE EVERY DAY." Well, that was the idea, anyway. As anybody in the construction business knows, there are factors that keep you from being able to work every day. As I think back on that project, I wonder where my life would have led me if I knew then what I think I know now.

After Southland Village, I thought I was a genius. So we jumped right into a subdivision called Lexington Green. There were a few challenges there that we didn't have to face in Southland Village. First, there was no commercial site to sell and raise money for the residential side of things. And second, we had to build a sewer system for the subdivision.

Perhaps the most interesting challenge in Lexington Green was the hermit who owned adjoining land. I mean an actual hermit; he had been living on the site since his father had given him the land 40 years earlier. Hermits, I discovered, have their own way of doing things and their own reasons for staying in a spot or leaving it. I spent many an afternoon sitting in the hermit's shack, which was only one junk-filled room, trying to get him to sell. Where was I going to suggest he move? Another patch of woods? I finally got it done, and today the hermit's property is a subdivision adjoining Lexington Green.

The biggest challenge building Lexington Green, however, was that the market crashed during the approval process. All the money I had made in Southland Village had to be sunk into Lexington Green, finishing out the lots where we had started building. We sold the remaining lots to another development company, and it developed a couple hundred single-family homes. The company was Edward Rose and Sons from Detroit, a large, successful homebuilder. According to Sheldon Rose, one of the four sons in the business, they didn't make any money. But not long after I sold to them, General Motors announced that they were building a body plant very near the site. I called Sheldon and told him he should send me roses. He said, "Roses? I was thinking of sending you a bomb!" Nothing was easy.

I learned a huge lesson in Southland Village and Lexington Green: If you have holding power, you can rarely lose money in real estate. I was in no position to hold onto those lots, so Edward Rose and Company—which had plenty of cash on hand—swooped in and got that land for a song. Cash is king. When you are forced to raise cash quickly, sometimes you have no choice but to make the only decision you can, and those are often dumb decisions. Holding power protects you from the stupid things you might do. Holding power makes you look like a genius.

I don't know how much money I made during that period. For me, it wasn't about money. It was about the number of houses I was building and how often my name was in print. And the more houses I built, the more often my name was printed. As I said earlier, I was never really one of the "in crowd" in school. Now I was beginning to hit my stride.

But dealing directly with homebuyers was about to drive me crazy. One rainy day at about 5 p.m., a customer called who had just moved into a new house he had bought from me for $9,950. "My basement has water in it," he said.

I knew the guy pretty well, so I joked, "For $9,950, what did you expect to have in the basement? Champagne?"

He didn't think it was as funny as I did. "You'd better get over here," he said.

When I got to the house, there was indeed water in the basement. Five feet of it, and still filling. It was winter, and the ground had been frozen when we built the house, so we hadn't been able to backfill the foundation. Our big mistake was letting the customer move in anyway. Now a quick thaw had caused a disaster. Water was surrounding the foundation, and it was clear that if we didn't do something, the concrete blocks of the foundation would collapse and the house would fall into the basement.

On a cold Michigan night, I called a house-moving firm in the city and pleaded with them to come out and get some timbers under the house immediately. They came and tried to push large timbers in from the side, but in order to get them low enough, they had to cut through the frost with a jackhammer. The pounding caused the plaster in the next-door neighbors' house to crack, and they came out yelling at me. Finally with cross-timbers, the house movers were able to get things under control.

My net worth at the time was about $5,000. Thankfully, the house was insured without a deductible. All I had to replace was the washer and dryer. However, it turned cold again and we still couldn't backfill. So we replaced the shattered blocks, dried everything out, and moved the family back in. I could stop paying their hotel bill.

Then about two weeks later, there was another thaw and the basement filled back up with water. We went through it all over again, including buying another washer and dryer. Finally, with my net worth reduced to about $1,000, the problem was solved. Yet again, I had been forced into a dumb decision because I didn't have ready cash. We should have backfilled before we moved the family back in, but I didn't feel I could keep paying their hotel bill. Sometimes circumstances, along with a good amount of wishful thinking, cause you to make bad decisions.

Another incident that I remember well was a time we had a house built, but in our rush to close the loan, forgot to connect to the septic tank. Do you know what happens when you flush a toilet and the vent to the roof becomes the outlet? I'll let you use your imagination.

I even built a house on the wrong lot, next door to the folks who actually owned the lot. We were on the wrong side. The neighbors waited without saying anything until the house was nearly complete. Then called to tell me, "Thank you." A trade and a few of my precious dollars solved that mess.

On a more fundamental level, I learned the vital lesson that I shouldn't try to do it all. I was platting, designing, financing, selling, and building. Now, I have learned to take on the parts of a business that we can do best and hand off the other parts to others who are better qualified. Trying to be all things for all people is a dangerous strategy.

I drove past that water-in-the-basement house a few years ago. It was still standing. That mess and a few more like it got me into the wholesale building business and out of dealing directly with homeowners. I started building and selling new houses to real estate brokers in small towns across Southern Michigan.

I was able to build houses efficiently enough to make a construction profit and still leave room for the real estate broker—the one who would be dealing with the buyer—to make a profit. So in the early '60s, my business shifted from building for homebuyers to building for brokers.

My professional life changed very quickly one day when I was driving around Adrian, Michigan, with a broker for whom I was building a couple of single-family homes. He pointed out a site and asked if I would be interested in building some apartments on it. It was nothing special, but I had a feeling it would be a good location, being on one of the town's major streets. It already had sewer and water. What else did I need?

It looked like a real opportunity to me. So I agreed. I entered into an option contract to purchase the land. There was just one problem: I needed to come up with a deposit of $100, and times were tight. I got the money from Marilyn's household account, because her checks took longer to clear than my business checks.

As soon as I had nailed down the contract, I went to Detroit to see Sheldon Rose at Edward Rose and Sons. It was the largest homebuilder in Michigan at the time. I asked

Sheldon if he wanted to be a partner in the apartment project. Sheldon agreed, so I set out to learn the business.

I went to Scholz Homes in Toledo, Ohio, and met with the CFO. I told him I wanted to learn the apartment business but didn't have much time to learn. He asked me how much rent I could expect to get for an apartment in Adrian and how many units could be built on the site. I really did not know so I picked a number. We crunched the numbers—four acres at an apartment density of 25 units an acre, 95 percent occupancy, minus expenses. He then asked how much the expenses would be. Once again I did not know, but he told me the lenders would accept 30 to 35 percent. He asked how much I needed to borrow. That was an easy one: I needed to borrow all of it. So we calculated the debt service and subtracted it from the operating income, and that's when my math failed me. "How do you subtract a big number from a small number?" I asked.

"Easy," he said. "You just raise the rents." Well, now I knew all I needed to know. I was in the apartment business. I had a partner with money, a *pro forma* with a positive bottom line, and the ability to build a stick construction building.

As it turned out, it wasn't that easy. I started talking to lenders and contractors, and things dragged on. This was a little more complex than building single-family homes. Time was running out; I had to get the deal done or lose my $100. Things were already looking bad, and then one afternoon Sheldon Rose called to tell me that they had decided not to invest in Adrian after all. It was a shock; there went Marilyn's money!

The same night, I was sound asleep when the phone rang. You may wonder how I could sleep with such a crisis swirling around me. It's actually easy: If every day you do something about everything you *can* do something about, you can train yourself not to worry about those things you *can't* do anything about. When I picked up the phone, I found I was talking to a Mr. Rosen who asked if I had an apartment site in Adrian. Yes I did, I told him. Mr. Rosen asked if I would consider selling it.

I had been sound asleep when the phone rang. But now, as you might imagine, I was wide awake.

"Well," I said, "My partners and I are getting ready to build a 100-unit apartment building on that site." Since the Roses had dropped out, perhaps I should have said, "My *as-yet-undetermined* partners and I are getting ready to build a 100-unit apartment building on that site." Details, details. I continued, "We've been lining things up, you know. Talking to builders and the banks." (I didn't mention that the banks' side of the conversation was one "no" after another). "But I don't know … I suppose it's possible that I would consider selling it if you made me the right offer."

"How soon could you meet me in Adrian?" Mr. Rosen asked.

"Let me look at my calendar," I said. "Hmmm … looks like I couldn't do it any earlier than 8:00 tomorrow morning."

Well, there was no chance of my sleeping any more that night. Now I had something I could do something about. I got right out of bed and drove the 90 miles to Adrian to be sure I arrived on time for our 8:30 meeting. I got there on time, all right—about five hours early.

We met at a restaurant, and Mr. Rosen bought my contract for $20,000. Cash. Just like that, I went from wondering how I was going to pay back Marilyn's $100 to sitting on $20,000 in cash. And I thought, "How long has this been going on without me?"

You've heard the saying, "The harder I work, the luckier I get." There's a certain amount of truth in that. It takes some effort to get in a position to be able to capitalize on any luck that might come along. But I'm not kidding myself. There are people who have worked as hard as I have—or even harder—and have less to show for it. I have enjoyed a lot of success in my life, but a lot of it came down to being in the right place at the right time. When I was about to lose Marilyn's $100 in the Adrian deal, it wasn't my hard work, intelligence, or merit that caused Mr. Rosen to pay me $20,000. It was luck. And there are times, as they say, when being lucky is better than being smart.

I'm not saying that business success is only about luck. It takes many things, including hard work, good sense, honesty, and a sense of fairness. But let's be honest: The difference between being successful and being wildly successful is mostly luck. Getting a good education, taking care of your health, working fairly and treating others the way you would like to be treated will guarantee you a great life in this incredible country called the United State of America. Getting to the next economic level of success is, in my opinion, mostly luck.

Think of it this way. Say you've got a stadium full of 100,000 people. They all flip a coin, and everybody who gets tails is out and everybody who gets heads stays in. After one round, you're down to 50,000. After two rounds, you're down to 25,000, 12,500 after three rounds, and 6,250 after four rounds. After 12 rounds, you're down to about 25 people out of the 100,000 who started. Those 25 people may believe that they are gifted coin-flippers; maybe they believe that they lead a charmed life. But they'd better not make any serious decisions based on their ability to flip heads; they've still got a 50 percent chance of flipping tails with every flick of the thumb. They're going to hit the wall eventually. Business decisions cannot be made with the flip of a coin.

With Mr. Rosen's $20,000, I was in the apartment-building business. And soon I had a goal that was even more ambitious than selling a house every 24 hours. I was determined to be the biggest apartment builder in the United States.

The ego trip was now rolling downhill and gaining momentum. With Edward Rose and Sons as a partner, we started building in Peoria, Illinois, and soon in Wichita, Kansas. Then I went on my own, building in Omaha, Nebraska, and Topeka, Kansas. Two friends and I bought a new four-place single engine Cessna 182 airplane for $18,000, all borrowed of course. I was the only employee in the company except for an on-site partner in Peoria.

Every Sunday night, after the kids went to bed, I left Kalamazoo in the airplane—which was soon replaced with a twin engine Cessna 310—and flew to Peoria. After a full Monday in Peoria, I left at night and flew to Topeka. I had an old Chevrolet that I parked by the fence at the airport in Topeka; every week I had to pump up the tires with the air hose from the fixed base operation. I spent Tuesday on the Topeka project, then again after dark, flew to Wichita, where I spent Wednesday and Thursday on another project before flying to Omaha on Thursday night. Friday night I flew back home, hopefully arriving in time for dinner with the family.

I kept the books for the company and wrote the checks to pay the bills while I was flying on autopilot at night; I had a special light hooked up over my seat. I did this every week for 14 months.

Then Marilyn and I decided to move to Wichita. While I was traveling every week, I built a house in Wichita. Marilyn only saw it one time while it was under construction. We lived there for more than 25 years.

While in Wichita, I bought a bright yellow car—the kind of car that everybody would notice—and parked it outside my office where everybody could see that I got to work before anyone else and was working hard to make my dream a reality. When people in Wichita drove to work in the morning, they could see that I was already in my office. When they drove home in the evenings, they could see that I was still at it. I knew that when I owned most of the world, people would say how hard I worked to get there. I even thought about buying another yellow car and leaving it at the office!

A few people noticed. A few mentioned that they saw the yellow car in front of my office at all hours. But the whole routine was really for the benefit of one person: my mother. I thought if I worked hard enough, then she would notice. I thought if I became the biggest apartment builder in the country, she would tell me she was proud of me. I thought if I owned the whole world, perhaps she would say, "I love you." Was this a reason to be in business? I don't think so.

When my mother was mostly confined to her bed, her two favorite nieces came to visit her in Wichita and Mom asked me to show them the city. I took a day off and did just that. After Betty and June left town, Mom said, "Thanks for spending the day with the girls. You know, I love you." Ironic, isn't it? After working so many thousands of hours to hear my mother say she loved me, it was taking the day off and spending time with family that finally made it happen. The lesson here is very clear. Priorities, priorities, priorities.

The "all about me" trip continued to grow. As I was building the apartment company, work consumed me. Since people couldn't really see my net worth, my goal became building 10,000 apartments per year. We had developed more than 16,000 apartments. I was the second largest apartment builder in the country. Oh, how I wanted to be first.

# Partners

Often, when you think about looking for a partner, you first think about the money, who gets what, and what you have to give to get the partner on board. My experience tells me that is backwards. Who your partner is has to be your first consideration. Remember, human nature is such that when the partner makes money and is happy, he will tell his friends how smart he is. If it is a less than expected return, he may tell his friends how bad *you* are. It's a no-win situation. What kind of a human being is this potential partner? Does the partner share your moral values? Can he afford to lose the money? Does he bring more than money to the deal? Now you can start thinking about the deal itself, but make sure everyone knows absolutely everything about the deal, good and bad. If you've held anything back, get it on the table early. Finally, have an exit strategy. The best way to do this is the so-called "Abe Lincoln." Either partner can set the price to buy or sell and the other partner chooses. Simple ... like two kids dividing a candy bar.

# A Passion for Airplanes

In the fourth grade, I wrote about my future. I wanted to be a doctor, but more importantly, I planned a series of hospitals and a fleet of airplanes and helicopters to travel between the buildings. My plan was to have people pay for health care before they were sick. That is an interesting concept. But it was the airplanes that really drove this dream. I have always wanted to be a pilot. Flying has been a lifelong passion of mine.

In the early days, having airplanes was mostly to show off my success. In my second business life, however, the airplanes have been great business tools. They have been a real joy to have and share with friends. Flying has been a wonderful escape from the business world for me. It is like being in another world. And the business of flying seems to attract wonderful people, many of whom have become good friends. My hero in the aircraft industry was Duane Wallace, who built Cessna from a failed airplane company into what it is today. Knowing Duane was a real highlight of my life. I was fortunate to meet and know Bill Lear, a genius who, among other things, invented the car radio, small plane autopilot, 8-track stereo, and of course, the now-famous Learjet. I have many great memories of spending time with Bill. They broke the mold after they made him. Our guys at Wichita Air Services have been together for more than 20 years, and we have always approached the flying business in a very professional way. The tales from all these 40-plus years of flying—including the time I set a world speed record for small

*(continued)*

51

jet aircraft—would fill another book. I guess the lesson here is to find a passion outside of your business and learn to enjoy it throughout your life.

I have bought and sold several airplanes in my life, and never for a profit. I have always said that there is no way to justify an airplane. It can only be rationalized. Thankfully, rationalization is something I do very well. So here's my rationalization: Late one afternoon just as we took off from LAX in our Learjet headed to Wichita, the phone in the plane rang. It was Bill Johnson, who was buying sites for Residence Inns. He told me there was a piece of land on Highway 101 south of San Francisco that we could buy if we could get there immediately and meet with the seller. As we climbed out, we turned left and headed for SFO. I met with the owner, signed the deal, and bought that land and a site nearby. As those deals unfolded and we built two Residence Inns, we made enough money to pay for all the airplanes we have owned. All of this because we had our own aircraft. How's that for a rationalization? Private airplanes are expensive, but so is time. In business, when you can extend the productivity of team members who have the ability to say yes and get things done, the price of using the airplane is no longer that important.

# Is your sales team making more money than you? Great!

People who sell stuff are of a special breed. Sales people in companies are often resented or looked down upon by other employees because they often make more money yet seem to be more freewheeling and carefree. They travel to fun places, eat nice dinners, go skiing and golfing with clients. No wonder those watching from behind a desk feel a little jealous.

In your business, you need to understand that salespeople are a special group who need to be led differently than most other employees. Compensating the sales types is really easy: Sell something, and you get paid; don't bring in business, and you get fired. The score keeping is easy, but the pressure on the sales person is huge. Therefore, the sales person needs to have the chance to make really good money. If your sales force is making more money than you are, that is a good sign. They are taking more upfront risk than any other employee in the company. And risk and return is a rule of life.

When you're putting together a compensation package for a salesperson, give a salary that is less than the amount needed to live comfortably. Then set up commissions on sales so that the salesperson gets a lower percentage of sales until your business overhead is covered, and a higher percentage of sales above that amount. That way, they can make really good money when they get the job done. After all, once your over-

*(continued)*

head is covered, your margins will increase at a much faster rate as more sales come in.

I have often run across business owners who don't want their sales teams making more money than they do. Without exception, their businesses did not grow to the potential they really could have. There was always turnover on those sales teams as really good salespeople moved on to greener pastures and the "ho hum, I am satisfied with what I have" types stayed around. I would love nothing better than to have a sales team whose members are making a million dollars a year!

# Some Simplifying Questions

Business ought to be pretty simple. Those around you will complicate everything as they try to impress you with all of their knowledge. Stay simple by keeping your main goals in mind as you think through the information you have. Here are some questions that will help you do that:

- What are you really trying to accomplish with this deal?
- How will it affect the future of your business?
- How will it affect the stakeholders and your employees?
- Will it complicate your real goals?
- Does it meet the moral commitments you have?
- When it is done, will it really make a positive difference to the business?
- What is the moral compass of the new players if the deal brings them to the table?
- Will you be able to make other deals for the right reasons going forward?
- Will the deal tie your hands going forward?
- Will the new players bring positive force to the business?
- Who will be in control when the deal is done?
- What are your personal goals going forward and does this deal meet or change them?
- Does this deal change the way you have to do business?
- Is that change positive?

*(continued)*

- What is the message you are sending to your employees and customers by doing this deal?
- Who are the players you may be inviting into your business? Do they fit?
- Is the effort required to do the deal going to add or detract from your main business efforts?

Pretty long list, but reread it and you can reduce every business decision to a simple question that can be decided upon quickly.

# 4

# The Apartments that Jack Built

Worrying too much about you in business blinds us to the realities of the world around us. Hope and optimism are one thing; you can't be an entrepreneur without them. But ego causes a businessperson to make decisions based on non-business factors. And the results can be disastrous. If you don't get control of yourself, eventually outside forces will do it for you, and you may not like the results.

"We try harder." Avis Rental Cars has one of the most recognizable slogans in all of the advertising world. It's been around so long, in fact, that a lot of people have forgotten its original context. Avis tries harder, the original campaign said, because Avis isn't number one. Always second fiddle to Hertz, Avis has no choice but to try harder. An ad from 1964 reads,

When you're not the biggest in rent a cars, you have
to try harder. We do. We're only number two.

At Jack P. DeBoer and Associates, we knew that feeling well.
We were always striving. We were only number two. I was fueled
by an irrational desire to overtake the country's top apartment
builder. Being number two is no fun. It certainly does nothing
for your ego.

We built hundreds of millions of dollars worth of apartments—millions of square feet. "The Apartments Jack Built,"
we called them. The apartment-building company spawned
a number of related companies in the late '60s and early '70s:
DeBoer Building Systems, DeBoer Travel, DeBoer Furniture
Leasing, DeBoer Construction, and more. I was putting my
name on anything that would stay still long enough for us to
slap a decal on—buildings, trucks, airplanes, forklifts, you name
it. That logo, by the way, was telling: a big "J" wearing a crown.
King Jack, Emperor of the Apartment Business and Related
Industries. In retrospect, I realize these efforts never really rented an apartment, which, of course, was the only important thing.

Every time we opened an apartment complex, we staged a
huge opening event. We wanted to make sure it was one of the
biggest parties of the year in whatever city we were building in.
We spent a lot of money on those parties. Did we get a return on
that investment? No, we didn't. But it wasn't about the money
at that time. It was about getting our name out. No, not our
name; it was about getting *my* name out—Jack P. DeBoer of
Jack P. DeBoer and Associates.

During that time, I always felt there must be a better way
to build. After all, the way we built—and still build—residential was, for the most part, the way building was done in my
grandfather's day. The differences are pretty superficial, mostly
involving more efficient ways to do the same things. We dig out
foundations with a backhoe whereas they dug them out with a
horse-pulled slip scraper. We use poured concrete for basement

walls whereas they used cement block. Our drywall has replaced their lath and plaster. We bring finished windows and doors to the job ready to install instead of building them on-site. But everything else is basically the same and has been for the last 100 years.

It struck me as old-fashioned and inefficient. How could a method that was good enough for my grandfather be good enough for Jack DeBoer of Jack P. DeBoer and Associates? For one thing, I felt there had to be ways to benefit more from our economies of scale. For a few years, I experimented with the core-and-panel method—basically a version of manufactured housing in which we built kitchens and bathrooms in a plant. We built a 100,000 square foot plant in Wichita, Kansas, bought a fleet of ten Peterbilt tractors, put the King Jack logo on everything, and used the system to build apartment projects as far west as Phoenix, Arizona. Oh, the thrill of watching 15 flatbed train cars with our panels and logo pulling out of the Wichita station!

The idea made a lot of sense. It was a way to control quality and speed up the construction process. More than that, it was a way to spread the big "J." A very dear friend ran DeBoer Building Systems. Fred Sopjes was from the lumber business and was my brother's brother in-law. He did everything right to deliver the product from engineering to construction in the field. What I did not realize was the need to keep a production line running smoothly day in and day out. The development business doesn't work that way. It is affected by so many outside forces that smooth production schedules simply aren't possible—at least not the level of smoothness that a manufacturing operation requires. DeBoer Building Systems closed. Boeing occupies the plant today.

By the way, no company has ever been successful long-term in prefabricating units for the residential world. No one. I knew it at the time, but I thought I was different. I had it in my head that I couldn't fail at anything I put my mind to.

Those apartment-building days were fat times. Money was easy to come by. REIT's (Real Estate Investment Trusts) were throwing money at us. I was moving steadily toward my goals, unhealthy and egocentric as they were. I wasn't the top apartment builder in the country, but I was closing fast on the guy who was. I had 2,000 employees throughout the country. We had built thousands of apartments—2,000 in Wichita alone. Everywhere I went in my new hometown, I could point to another apartment that Jack built.

In the late '60s and early '70s, when we were pushing hard to get to 10,000 apartment starts a year, my good friend Jack Bertoglio in Kansas City decided he was ready to sell his company, Gold Crown Inc. He was a building contractor, and we had partnered on a few garden apartment projects. Jack had been profitable for a few years, but he wanted to increase his volume in order to bulk up earnings to get a higher price for his company.

We had five projects in the pipeline, so we contracted with Jack to get the construction done. We knew that Redman, a public company, was going to make him an offer, so the extra projects helped him out. Jack had a great track record of coming in under budget and helping his partners make a profit, so it was a win-win all the way around. Jack got a higher price for his company, and Redman had five good projects in the pipeline when they bought Gold Crown.

But right about that time, trouble appeared on the horizon for everybody in the development business. I was starting to see signs of trouble for my company, then Redman began to struggle and wasn't able to complete the properties we had contracted them to build. It was a multi-million dollar mess: They couldn't keep building without getting cash from us, but we couldn't afford to give them more cash without seeing a little more progress. We worked really hard to settle, and at last we came to within $50,000 of one another. In one sense we were really close; $50,000 is a lot less than $1 million. But at that point in my life, $50,000 was a lot of money—more than I could come up with—and I didn't feel that I owed it. Having come that close, neither one of us was budging.

Carl Summers, who had worked for Jack at Gold Crown, was now in charge of completing the projects for Redman. I had known Carl longer than anybody else at Redman. He suggested that we flip a coin to settle our impasse. I agreed and the folks at Redman agreed. The lawyers looked pretty surprised when we told them we had decided to flip a coin. They told us we had to flip the coin in Las Vegas, where gambling was legal. I think they just wanted to get a paid trip to Las Vegas.

So we set a date and time to meet in Vegas. I flew out with a couple of guys and our lawyer the night before we were to meet. That was a restless night. I had a 50-50 chance of owing $50,000 that I simply didn't have.

The next morning, we met in a big banquet room at the Hilton—one with a 16-foot ceiling, the better to flip a coin. According to the contract we wrote, Carl was to bring a silver dollar, I was to flip it, and he was to call heads or tails.

All eyes were on Carl and me as we stood in the middle of the room. $50,000. One coin flip. My stomach was in knots. As Carl handed me the coin, it was as if a flash of reason lit up the whole room. I suddenly understood how crazy this scenario was. "Let me buy this silver dollar from you," I said.

Carl looked at me, confused. "Buy the silver dollar?"

"Yeah. I'll give you $25,000 for this coin. We'll call it settled. We'll walk away. What do you say?"

Carl thought on it. He couldn't afford to lose $50,000 any more than I could. Neither of us felt we could afford to lose $25,000 either, but at least we could cut our losses. It seemed like 15 minutes he stood there weighing my offer. I just about rubbed the eagle off the back of that dollar, I was so nervous. Finally Carl broke into a grin. "That makes sense, Jack," he said. "You give me $25,000 for that dollar, and we've got a deal."

The others in the room begged me to flip the coin and Carl to call it just so they would know what would have happened.

"No way," I said. No good could have possibly come from that.

To this day, I have a framed photo in my office of Carl and me standing in the middle of that room at the Las Vegas hotel. Below the photo is the actual coin that I bought for $25,000, and below that are the words, "LET REASON PREVAIL." It was a little moment of sanity in a season of craziness for me. Unfortunately, even though reason prevailed in that one instance, it would be a while yet before reason prevailed for good.

---

The peak of my egomania came in 1970, when the Singer Corporation (as in Singer sewing machines) offered $100 million of Singer stock for Jack P. DeBoer and Associates. In 1971, $100 million was a lot of money. I thought about the offer a little while, but I didn't have to think hard. A rival of mine had recently received $100 million for his company. I couldn't stand the thought of going to a national convention and having people say, "Oh, look, there's Jack DeBoer. Did you know he got a $100 million for his company TOO?" It was that "TOO" that I couldn't tolerate. No, I had to be number one.

The Singer Corporation market cap was $1.6 billion. Surely they could pay me more than $100 million. If they would bump it up to $160 million, I could tell my friends that I owned ten percent of Singer. And while they were at it, why shouldn't a ten percent owner be on the board? Yes, I was that crazy. Somebody should have put me in the nuthouse. I made my unreasonable demands, and the deal fell through.

How much did I value my ego? The math is pretty easy. I was 95 percent owner of the company (the Ford Foundation owned the other five percent). So I valued my ego somewhere north of $95 million. And those were 1970 dollars.

Six months later, I was broke. Not bankrupt; I've never declared bankruptcy. But I was completely broke. I owed money to hundreds of creditors affecting thousands of people, almost all of it bills due on projects under construction. Interest rates were in the high teens to low 20's. I had bitten off more than I could chew. Those were the go-go days when subcontractors doing big dollar contracts had a net worth of almost nothing. If they got tired of waiting for money, they simply left the job and went elsewhere. As I ran out of money to pay contractors on time, the slide to financial failure accelerated and, as described in the prologue of this book, dark days were soon upon me.

Egomania is a disease that is almost impossible to self-diagnose. After all, when you're in the middle of it, it doesn't feel like a disease. To put it another way, going 100 miles an hour on a self-driven run is pretty exhilarating ... until you hit a wall. And when you're in the grips of "me, me, me," you're going to hit the wall eventually, as it forces you to take more risks and go faster just to feed it.

I suppose I know everything there is to know about ego, so what are the signals? I was blinded to the real world I was living in. When you live in your own fantasy world, who needs the real world anyway? Ego plugged my ears, turning me into a non-listener. When you have all the answers, why would you need to listen to anybody else? It is a self-contained Peter Principle: It causes you to elevate yourself and everyone around you to your and their own level of incompetence. The irony is that the more you're satisfied with yourself as the object of other people's respect, the less people respect you. Think about the egomaniacs you know; you might respect what they've accomplished, but don't you find it hard to respect them as people? As I think back, I am convinced that I would not have liked me.

I mentioned earlier that ego can have a blinding effect. In my case, it blinded me to some of the most fundamental principles of business. When I looked at my balance sheet, I treated a dollar of fixed assets (especially real estate) as equivalent to a dollar of current assets (i.e., cash). That was the big mistake that led to my undoing. I made decisions based on the assumption that I could predictably convert fixed assets to cash. But when the interest rates soared and the REIT's soured, it was impossible to know what the assets were worth if you had to sell. Everything about that equation changed, and I simply wasn't ready for it. I had been treating my hopes and expectations as if they were reality.

Many times in the past, reality outstripped my hopes and expectations. I had come to believe that the translation of a $100 option into a $20,000 payday was just the way things went for me. I believed that God was smiling on me in a special way. So I kept taking on more risk in spite of facts that now seem obvious. Interest rates were approaching all-time highs, but I kept borrowing. If I had been thinking straight, I would have seen Singer's offer as a miraculous opportunity to be rescued from my crazy over-extension. But no. I had the insane goal of building 10,000 apartments in a single year. And the REIT's were still throwing money at apartment developers. So, to my way of thinking, why not keep charging ahead?

What was happening was I was making business decisions based on non-business concerns. I was looking for my business to give me something that business simply cannot give. My self-worth was so enmeshed with the balance sheet that I could no longer read it.

Maybe that's why it's called a balance sheet—because you have to have a certain amount of balance to be able to read it. You have to be able to separate the concerns of that sheet from the concerns that don't, in the end, have anything to do with the financial condition of your company.

I sometimes wonder what would have happened if I had just taken Singer's $100 million offer. But I think I know now what would have happened. The insane treadmill would have continued. I would have continued to take greater and greater risks. Eventually, I would have lost more than money and been unable to recover. Until I dealt with my issues, the crash was inevitable. And without the crash, I would have never been able to move from ego to humility. Keep in mind that the biggest comfort at the bottom was that the only thing I had really lost was money, and there was a very good chance that I could get that back.

Egomania may be hard to self-diagnose, but the time comes when no amount of blindness can hide the fact that you've headed down the wrong path. The time comes, in other words, when you finally hit the wall. For me, the wall came in the form of the "pay me Friday, or I'll kill you" phone call.

I've started, invested, or been involved in a lot of companies, and most of them have failed—they didn't make money. Neither I nor any of my businesses have ever gone bankrupt or been foreclosed on, but I have had a lot of businesses come close. And here's one thing I've learned through all those failures: When you're starting or purchasing a business, the positives are a lot easier to see than the negatives, especially for the optimist. And isn't every entrepreneur an optimist? The negatives become obvious later—usually after you've stopped walking on water and find yourself swimming in the lake. The challenge is to identify on the front-end all the things that can go wrong. Consult with the best people you know and listen to what they have to say. Work to get to the most negative view of the thing you're about to do. Then ask yourself, "Does this still make sense?" And, by the way, it might still make sense to move forward even if the prospects aren't as rosy as you had first thought. Business is a matter of risk. Just make sure you're only risking money and not your family, health, friendships, reputation, or anything else that is difficult or impossible to get back. Money—you can get that back easily enough. It's made for risking. Oh, have I said that before?

# Naming Your Company

The guys on the Saturday morning "Car Talk" radio program joke that they are represented by the law firm "Dewey Cheetham and Howe" (say it out loud, and you'll get the joke). Which makes me think, why do people who start businesses put their names on the door in the first place? Does your name tell a potential customer what you do? Not unless your name happens to be Plumber or Electrician or Insurance Broker. Do you think having your name on the door will bring in more customers? Probably not. I know why I put my name on my company and by now, you know as well.

If you're starting a new company, my advice is to consider almost any other name for your company besides your own. I realize it's a headache to have to vet company names to be sure you don't infringe on somebody else's. But it's worth it; you don't want to be making business decisions geared toward promoting your personal name. That separation is important. Find a name that you can protect nationally; you never know, you might be national someday, and having to change it would be an expensive hassle. And be sure you can get the .com, .net, and .org URL's for your new company name.

# Dealmakers and Flakes

Let me tell you about dealmakers and flakes. I once listed all of the people I did business with and came up with a startling fact: Everybody in the business world is either a dealmaker or a flake. If you list dealmakers on one side of the page and flakes on the other, you won't have to think twice about which column to put anybody in. And you will never, ever move a name from one column to the other.

Why do we do business with flakes? Because they're fun! Let's say you're struggling in your business, and you've got some wild dream that's going to save you, and you say to your banker, "Here's my wonderful dream." If he's a dealmaker, he's going to say, "Get out of my office. Come back when you're ready to talk sense." But if he's a flake, he's going to say something like, "I think that's wonderful. Let's go even higher together." And you'll say, "Gee, what a great experience I'm having!" But your flaky banker isn't actually a real business ally (and he won't lend you the money anyway).

So if you dare, make that two-column list. Go out and have a good time with the flakes, but only do business with dealmakers.

# Mentors and Confidantes

YPO (Young Presidents Organization) invited me
to join shortly after I moved to Wichita. Meeting four
to six times a year with the members was a great way
to learn what other business presidents were doing.
To qualify for YPO, you have to be the president of a
midsized to larger business with a minimum number of
employees and under the age of 45. At the time I was
involved, you couldn't continue with the organization
once you turned 50 years old. In addition to planned
education meetings, it offers social opportunities with
chapters around the world as well as International
University meetings.

The most valuable part of YPO, however, is what
is called YPO Forum. Each chapter has forum groups
of about ten members that meet monthly. My forum
group decided to continue meeting after we, because of
reaching 50 years, were out of YPO.

We have met quarterly for the past 25 or 30 years.
The purpose of Forum is to offer a place where members can talk openly about their problems and successes. Forum is confidential and discussions inside
are never discussed on the outside. In the early days
of Forum, discussions were about our business issues
and children. As we have aged, the subject has moved
to estate planning and grandchildren as well as health
issues.

Keep in mind that we are not going through this life
alone. If we're having one of those touchy, feely meetings, we soon learn that everyone in the room has, is
or will be going through the same struggles, albeit at
different intensity levels.

The point is, do not try to go through life alone. Get involved in some kind of formal meeting structure with people you can trust and where you can honestly discuss your personal issues. If all of your members are businessmen, then the group will focus on business issues for the most part. It is the business equivalent of a small church group discussing their faith.

I love the eight members of our forum and would trust each with my pocket book. And although I do not see most of them between meetings, I know they are there for me if I need them.

What a blessing.

Part II:
Success

# 5

# The Gift of Failure

*s much as we strive for success, sometimes the greatest gift turns out to be failure. It is failure, not success, that forces us to face the realities of who we are, who we have become, and who we might yet be. The businessperson who pays attention will find great riches and wisdom in the ruins of failure. My gift of failure was simply moving me from my false sense of myself to real humility.*

Hundreds of creditors. Interest rates in the high teens to low 20's. I was in a state of temporary insanity in the early '70s. I was in business to get huge, not to make money. I believed that doing the deal was most important. When you start thinking that way, each decision is made to cover the bad decision before it. You make a deal, get up-front money, and keep the doors open a while longer, but all you're really doing is delaying the inevitable. That's only wishful thinking. You're counting on a future you can't predict rather than the resources you have at hand; eventually the house of cards can't support itself any longer.

I've already mentioned the man who called and threatened to kill me if I didn't pay him. That's what I call a wake-up call. It was a moment when reality crashed in on the imaginary world I had created for myself.

Did I take it seriously? You bet I did. Outside my office for about a week, a friend kept watch with a gun, just in case my caller decided to try to make good on his threat. Of course, he didn't come to my office, nor did he ever call back. I guess he was just blowing off steam. I hope it did him some good. It sure did me some. Finally I realized the seriousness of being in business. When you make a promise, it immediately affects the lives and businesses of many others up and down the line. They make promises based on your promise, and the next people down the line make promises to even more people. It is an endless chain reaction. Many do not understand the far-reaching consequences of each and every business decision and promise.

At that time, putting a company into bankruptcy only required three creditors. We kept watch at the courthouse to see if any of my creditors were going to force us into involuntary bankruptcy. Bankruptcy, I knew, wasn't an option for me. I couldn't bear the public shame of it. I had made plenty of mistakes in my business, but I always had a reputation for honesty. To declare bankruptcy would be to tell people who had trusted me, "Sorry, pal ... that's what you get for trusting a guy like me." As I lay in my darkened bedroom and pondered the real possibility of going bankrupt, I wondered whether I could muster the courage to fly my airplane into the side of a mountain. To me, that seemed a better option than facing people after declaring bankruptcy. Just the thought of a *Wichita Eagle* headline reading, "Jack P. DeBoer and Associates Bankrupt" was all it took to keep me awake.

I had fun building the company. It had been a good run, but it had come to an end. How could I ever solve this problem? It literally seemed like it would be a superhuman task. I was standing on new ground: a new world that had nothing to do with my worth as a human being, business growth, or headlines.

But then it hit me: I may have been way short on money, but I still had some pretty significant assets. I had real estate that was going to be a part of the solution. But the real estate was nothing compared to other, less tangible assets. God had given me an environment to grow up in where I had worked every day to keep my word, and I understood that truth, no matter how painful, was the easiest and best way to run both my life and business. I had a hard-earned reputation for doing what I said I was going to do. We had a good reputation of paying our bills on time until we hit the wall. We never directly used anyone else's money. That reputation was going to be key to getting me out of this mess. I needed to stay the course, not bail out. I was learning the hard way that success was not permanent. But a new realization was dawning on me: Failure doesn't have to be permanent either.

It didn't feel like it at the time, but failure was a huge gift to me. Failure focused my attention and energy. Failure made me think seriously about what I could actually count on. Failure made me get creative again and serious instead of throwing money at a problem. Failure made me ask myself, "Do you have what it takes to do this, or don't you?" I convinced myself that I did have what it would take, including good energy and health.

I had dug myself a deep hole. Climbing out of it was going to be extremely difficult. But I had a strong wife who was—and still is—by my side. And I had gotten the ego blown right out of me. It was time for me to separate the personal issues from the business issues, batten down the hatches, forget about growing the country's largest apartment business and the dream of being a big deal, get my priorities straight, and get serious about making good to whom I owed money. Yes, I had made some promises I couldn't keep. But those promises were about money, not about my character or personal relationships. And here's the best news of all: Because I had kept those non-monetary promises, I was eventually going to be able to make good on the financial promises.

On February 2, 1973, I gave a speech to all my employees about what was going to happen. It was hard explaining to people who had trusted me that I couldn't guarantee that they would have jobs for much longer. As I prepared to write this part of the book, I looked back over my notes for that speech. I used words and phrases like *attitude, can-do, history, goals,* and *savings.* But more interesting than my speech notes were other notes that I found attached to them—hand-written notes that I received from employees.

"I believe in you."

"Keep the faith."

"I'm behind you 110%!"

"How can I help (25 hours a day)?"

"After sleepless nights, I now know that I really care about this company and the people."

"My loyalty is to Jack DeBoer, who is the company."

"I will stay with this company until they lock the doors and push me out."

"Proud to be a part of this team."

"Reduce my salary 10 percent as of February 1."

The turnaround I was embarking on wouldn't have been possible without that kind of support. As soon as the tears dried, I drew a lot of strength from comments like those.

---

When a businessperson (or anyone else) gets into a financial mess, the first question that almost always springs to mind is, "Where can I borrow the money to pay off these creditors and buy myself more time?" When you do that, you're only kicking the can a little further down the road. That kind of strategy almost never pays off in the long run. The best place to owe money is to where you already owe money. This is a lesson you should never forget. You already have a relationship with the people you owe money to. Hopefully they know from your actions during the good times to expect honest treatment from you. If they do, they're going to be much easier to work with than a new creditor.

Borrowing new money will always be more expensive and will never be enough to solve all the problems. If you borrow from a new source, some creditors will be left behind as you serve a new master. Borrowing new money will always dig a deeper hole. You will be asked to pledge the family, your wife or husband, your home. Keeping your family out of your business financial messes is another important rule. During my entire business life, I never let my wife sign any guarantees. You will always be asked, but if you agree not to transfer assets to your spouse while the loan is outstanding, you can usually avoid this. You probably can't avoid having both spouses' names on your home mortgage, but make it your rule not to have your spouse sign anything else.

After I decided to get out of bed and get on with my life, one of the first things I did was contact each of my creditors and give them a plan for paying the money I owed them. They weren't going to get the money by when they originally expected, but they were going to get it. This is where my earlier reputation for integrity really paid off. My creditors were willing to work with me because they knew that the only way they would ever get paid was if I stayed in business to pay them. And they knew that I had always been good for the money I owed. I was honest with them and explained that things had to happen for me to keep my promises going forward. It was clear that the only way for them to get their money was for me to succeed in getting it straightened out.

In each of the payment agreements I made, I was conservative in my estimate of how much and how quickly I could pay. It's so tempting to over-promise in a situation like the one I was in. You feel that you're in a weak position; you feel embarrassed; you feel that you've got something to make up, something to prove. So you stretch your estimates of what you can pay. But that only makes things worse, because the month will come when you can't pay what you promised. Once you break the new promise, your credibility starts to erode.

Somehow I had the wisdom to promise small payments stretched out over a relatively long period of time. Where I thought I could pay $1,000 a month, I promised to pay $500. Were my creditors disappointed with the timetable? Maybe. Or maybe not. Getting paid slowly is a whole lot better than not getting paid at all or only getting a fraction of payment. If I had gone bankrupt, that's what those creditors would have gotten. So even if they were a little disappointed at my long schedule, they weren't nearly as disappointed as they would have been with a missed payment. And on those months when I could pay $750 to the guy I had promised $500, my creditors were downright giddy and my personal credibility increased—not to mention how good it felt to do better, even if it was a small amount. It helped build my personal strength to keep going.

My problems totaled millions of dollars, but many of my debts were in the thousands. Those smaller creditors were generally the ones I promised monthly payments to. To the major creditors, I promised payment when deals were done. Those promises all depended on getting a project sold. I had to be careful not to let wishful thinking take over again; otherwise, I would have been back at the table trying to keep things calm instead of spending my time working on solutions. As I think back on those days, I take great comfort in realizing that I never thought about what I might have left when everyone was paid. Remember, when you are working your way out of a financial mess, you must always put yourself in second place.

We naturally think of the guy who owes money as being the weaker party. But it's not true. The guy who owes money is actually in a strong position. He's already gotten what he wants;

now it's the other guy who wants what the debtor has. I don't say that in order to encourage you to intentionally incur debts you can't repay. Your strong negotiating position evaporates quickly if you don't pay what you owe. But in those situations when you can't pay due to circumstances beyond your control—or even in situations where you've made an honest mistake—it helps to remember that, if you're serious about making things right with your creditor, you're in a stronger bargaining position than you think. After all, your creditors can't come to your office and write themselves a check. Nor do we have debtor prisons in this country.

When you don't have the money to pay your bills on time—and it happens to almost everybody at one time or another—remember, you know it before your creditor knows it. Deal with the situation before your creditor even knows there *is* a situation. *You* need to make the call and say, "Hey, I'm not going to be able to pay on time. Can we work out a plan?" You should never have to dread the ringing of the phone. Every time the phone rings, you are reminded that you are not making do on your promises. If you are fulfilling the negotiation you made with your creditors, then you can focus on working your way out of the hole. This might be the most important lesson to learn about solving money problems.

It's important to pay off or reach agreement with the smaller debts first. Economists and finance experts say it's more important to first pay down the debts with higher interest rates. That may be true strictly from a numbers perspective, but psychologically, it's important to get the smaller debts paid off, and then apply that freed-up money to your larger debts. It feels good to check off a debt, to have a shorter list of creditors this month than you had last month. The sense of accomplishment keeps you going and helps you stay the course even when it's hard. The few dollars you may earn by paying according to interest rate aren't worth it … with the exception of the usurious rates on credit cards. In this instance, get them paid or renegotiated as soon as possible. No matter how tight things get, never use the credit card to solve money problems. If you can't pay your balance monthly, cut up the card immediately.

There are many reasons why it's important to pay faithfully according to your negotiated agreement. Having the reputation of doing what you say you will do is, of course, a major step along the way to a successful business. There are, however, other clear economic advantages. Let's say you've signed a contract with a construction company, and the draw is due on a Friday. You could delay payment until Monday. It doesn't make any real difference to the construction company because it wouldn't deposit the money until Monday anyway. But in my company, I insist that we move heaven and Earth to pay on Friday if the contract payment date falls on a Friday. Why? Because I want to send a message that we do what we say we're going to do, and we expect our contractors to do what they say they're going to do. Intentionally using a creditor's money for personal gain is a clear signal that you are not an A player in the business world. Sooner or later, this and the little things you get away with will change who you are. If doing that sort of thing is what is keeping your business afloat, you're broke already. Fix it.

Another huge lesson to remember: In contracts, be careful to only take on things over which you have control. I tell our construction folks that when they sign a contract, take on only one commitment: to pay on time.

Also, as in my business, when you have the reputation of being fanatical about paying on time, you can negotiate better pricing. If a businessperson knows he can count on your cash flow, he's willing to cut you a break. The people he knows to be slower payers will have to pay a premium. Also, that person will begin to prioritize your progress milestones because he knows that's money in the bank. Your jobs stay on schedule.

In the construction business—just as in other industries—when your subcontractors and vendors know how you pay, they will treat you accordingly.

Some big and wealthy companies delay payment as a method of building cash. They rob Peter to pay Paul. The payee or the vendor can usually go to his bank and pledge the account receivable because it is pretty certain they will get paid eventually. However, borrowing money against money that is owed to them is very expensive, and if these same subs can find other work that pays on time, they will be gone in a second.

When strong companies delay payments to their vendors, the vendors find ways to make up the difference so they have cash flow while the big guy uses their money. Keep in mind that your vendors know more about what they do than you ever will. If you create an environment without trust, you will take more time to manage the account and in the end, the vendor may well take advantage of you in other ways. Show you can be trusted, deal with people you can trust, and life will be less complicated and a lot more fun.

For years, a huge U.S. retailer was notoriously slow to pay, managing payments carefully and cash for return. It was able to do this because many of its vendors found themselves totally at its mercy.

In the meantime, that retailer and many other large companies found that they couldn't always play the slow-pay game. To keep prices low, they provide cash to good vendors who give good prices but need operating capital. In other words, even the biggest guys will give a break to vendors who have dealt honestly with them, and both parties win. The vendor is a better businessman, and the customer gets better service and better prices.

---

After I got my head screwed on straight, I thought hard about what it was that allowed me to get out of a deep mess and turn my business life around. With a list of 25 or 30 specific things, none of which was money, I committed to share my experience with college and high school students and business people as often as I could. I committed to a policy that, if possible, I would never turn down an invitation to share the things I learned the hard way. I have made several hundred such talks over the past 25 years. I sure wish somebody had told me the things I tell those students ... though I'm not sure I would have listened! Most of those lessons are scattered throughout this book along with a related business experience. This allows you to understand where they came from and why they apply to any business.

I always tell students that successful business is basically honesty. And when I do, I get a lot of "yeah, right" looks from students. Students these days grew up hearing about Enron, MCI-Worldcomm, Countrywide Mortgage. Every show on television seems to portray businesspeople as either shady in their business dealings or immoral in their personal lives. So we are sending messages to young people that dishonesty is the order of the day in the business world. You know the old saying: People under 30 who are not liberal should have their heart examined, but once they pass 30, if they are still liberal, they should have their head examined. And many people, for some reason, think that business is fundamentally dishonest. I have news for people who think that way: Businesses that survive are honest. Period.

We all know about Enron, Global Crossing, MCI, and Countrywide, but they're aberrations. That's what makes them newsworthy. They're also no longer in business. There are more than 11,000 public companies in this country; the ones that make the news are the few that don't follow the rules. "Public Company Pays Taxes, Takes Care of Employees, Doesn't Cheat Anybody, Is Doing Fine." Not the most riveting newspaper headline, is it? But it's the real story of business in this country. The lesson here is simple: If you want to be in business, join the vast majority of successful businesses and act like they do.

Anybody who thinks a business, large or small, can keep up a web of lies for long has never spent much time doing business. Dishonesty is a serious brain drain. Every person has a brain about the same size, wired differently for sure, but about the same size. The challenge is to use that brain in a positive and meaningful way. If you spend your brain time worrying about covering up your lies, you will have no time to use it for the good things in your life. It is true that some people are smarter than others and will be able to get away with lies longer, but sooner or later every liar gets his comeuppance.

Truth is so easy. You don't have to have a memory if you tell the truth. A whole section of your brain is available to you for other things. Often, we think that the best reason for telling the truth is that it's what our parents or the church taught us. There's nothing wrong with that. But on a much more prag-matic level, in business you need to tell the truth because it's the only way to be successful. The good news is that telling the truth works in every part of your life. Truth is a huge gift, and it's free.

When I pulled myself up from being flat on my back, I had determination and drive. But the determination, drive, and even my real estate holdings wouldn't have been enough to get me out of my hole if I hadn't already earned the trust of people in the past. As I said earlier, if only three of my creditors had wanted to see me fail, if only three of them had had it in for me, I would have failed. If just a few people had said, "No, I won't work with you ... I'll see you in court!" it would have been over for me. Just a few people saying that I was dishonest or a dead-beat would have been hard for me. It would have taken away my drive to get back up. Yes, who you are is so much more impor-tant than what you are or what you have.

In my recovery from failure, I was a little surprised at how many of the same people wanted to do business with me again. I have asked some of those people why they were willing to give me another chance, when it was perfectly clear that my failure was my fault, that my ego had been completely out of control. The answer: "You always told the truth." Our companies do business with many of those companies and banks today.

We all make stupid mistakes. We all need forgiveness and a second chance every now and then. You're going to find that your forgiveness and second chances come a lot easier when you have a reputation for telling the truth. Truth covers a multitude of sins. When things go wrong and you have done something you are not proud of, a reputation for telling the truth earns you the right to simply say, "I made a mistake and I am sorry."

Lie to me once, and I will never be able to believe you again. Forgive and forget? That's one ideal that doesn't apply to business, politics, or other aspects of public life. The vast majority of people tell the truth, and I don't feel the need to deal with liars. A few years ago, I wanted to have a boat built. I was trying to decide between several boat yards that seemed equally qualified. I narrowed it down to three yards; the one I favored sent a representative to talk further about a possible contract. During the negotiation he told me something that I knew to be absolutely false. End of negotiation. It wasn't a huge lie, but we were about to enter into a long, complex process. There were things ahead that I had no personal knowledge of, things I would have to take this man's word on. I couldn't afford to risk millions of dollars in a situation where I wasn't sure I could trust the other party. One small falsehood cost that boat yard a multi-million-dollar contract.

When people say of you, "You can take what he says to the bank," life becomes very easy. Deals get done. Truth is an investment. Like any investment, it can be hard to pay on the front end. It's tempting to take the easy way out and let the future take care of itself. But truth is like other investments in another way: you benefit from a compounding effect. Small pay-ins—telling the truth in little things that don't seem to matter very much—become big payouts as time goes on. Hopefully you don't have to draw on your "truth account" very often, but when you need to—when, for instance, you have to start over again after failure—you're very glad it's there.

# The Value of Humility

People know it when you have success, position, money, toys, good health, and friends in high places. Nothing is more boring than a person who constantly reminds others of what they have or have achieved, how healthy they are, who they know, how far they ran this morning, how big their boat is, or what kind of airplane they have.

Humility is so much more appealing than chest thumping. Just remember, with a few important exceptions like personal relationships, almost everything you have is fleeting. You could easily lose it. Then what? You may need some help, that's what. And arrogance isn't going to help. Arrogance doesn't build anything. Arrogance doesn't draw anybody together. Arrogance only pushes people away and says, "I don't need you." We may wish we didn't need anybody, but the truth is, we all do. My good friend Fred Fetterolf, past president of Alcoa, reminded me that being humble and meek is very different from being weak.

A humble man can draw on his personal resources when he needs help. We all fail. We all need help at some time or another, and when we do, we realize that we aren't going through this life alone. Building a bank of good deeds for others will serve you well in times of need. Arrogance draws down your balance more quickly than almost anything else. Does this sound like a selfish approach to humility and good deeds? No, it's just practical.

# Don't Tell Me How Honest You Are ... Show Me

I make it a practice not to trust anybody who keeps telling me how honest he is. Honesty is a way of life, not a bunch of lip service. It's a little bit like being pregnant: either you are or you aren't. There's no such thing as "sort of honest" or "mostly honest." Like so many things in your life, you can spend a lifetime getting the reputation of being honest, only to have that reputation destroyed by one stupid act.

One of the most difficult business types to assess early is the person who wears his faith on his sleeve. I'm not talking about at church or in a volunteer situation. I'm talking about an environment where money is involved. There have been situations in which I've seen a person's true colors too late. In a new business relationship, have you ever had someone work really hard to make sure you know how strong his faith is? I don't want to sound cynical, but more often than not, I've found that people who do that aren't so much expressing their faith as hiding behind it—as if God-talk were some kind of substitute for real character.

When you're interviewing a job applicant, it's against the law for you to ask questions about religious faith. It's supposed to protect the applicant, but, I think it's a protection for the employer too. In business settings, religious talk is as likely to conceal as to reveal. A person who is truly driven by his faith won't have to tell you about it. It will be easy enough to see from his actions.

# The Power of Fairness

When you're in a financial pickle, it may be tempting to tell yourself that your difficulties give you an excuse to cut corners—to look out for you at the expense of people you owe money to. It feels like the other guy holds all the cards ... so why shouldn't you stick it to him a little bit if you think you can get away with it? After all, he's going to be looking out for himself. It is extremely important in that situation to hold yourself to as high a standard as ever. Don't think about how much you can get for yourself; think only about being fair to the creditor and working together to solve the problem. If you send signals that you want to gain at the creditor's expense, the negotiations could shut down and you probably won't like the outcome. Instead, think along the lines that your problems are really the creditor's problems too. Think of yourself as working alongside the creditor. Think win-win. You'll get out of the mess eventually, and then you can worry about yourself a little bit more. Meanwhile, bend over backwards to be fair to your creditors.

As I think back about those really tough times, I've forgotten most of the details. That's a good thing. What I do remember is that I was fair and truthful. And that has been a source of great pride and happiness throughout the rest of my life. Fairness and integrity are two of the most important tools when you have to work your way out of trouble.

# A Second Chance

I have often gone to the State Prison in Hutchinson, Kansas, to talk to inmates who have a chance at parole the next year. It has been an amazing experience to talk to a room of 100 to 200 hundred men, all of whom need a second chance. My message is always the same: "Don't go back to your old ways and friends. Get a new start." And I always get the same question: "How do I get a new start? Who will help me?"

I tell them that I am not a bank, but that I will meet with them and help direct them to a job. I give my card to any of them who ask. You would be amazed at how few actually follow up. But some do, including a man named Willie. He sent me an eight-page, handwritten letter in which he said he wanted a new start so he could show his parents he wasn't a bad person.

I contacted the prison official who had set up the program and gotten me involved. He told me that Willie had been a model prisoner and that I might actually be able to help him. So I drove to Hutchinson and met with Willie in the warden's office for more than an hour while the warden paced outside the door.

Meth had taken all but two or three of Willie's teeth, so he wouldn't smile. But I could tell he was serious about making a new start. I told him I would be willing to help him get a job with one of our hotels in Wichita. I told the warden that I was going to help Willie, and she arranged for his early release to the Wichita work release facility. Willie went to work for the Hotel at Old Town. The staff put their arms around him and taught him basic painting and maintenance. He once told me the thing he liked best about his job was being able to talk to the guests because they did not know who he was. That's a sad thing to think about—a man whose self-esteem is so low that he prefers the company of strangers.

I told Willie that he had to have his teeth fixed so he could smile. With a lot of coaching, he finally went to my dentist, had the remaining teeth pulled and was fitted with false teeth. The team at Charles Squires Dental Clinic always ask about Willie. They truly care. Thanks to the help and care of co-workers and others, Willie has gotten on his feet and become a person who doesn't mind being known by people.

Willie moved to Florida to be near his aging parents. I loaned him some money to buy a car, and every month he makes his payments—on time, I might add. Margaret Potter, my assistant, talks to Willie every couple of weeks. He is still working and doing well.

My point is not to brag about putting a man on the straight and narrow. I didn't. Willie got his life on track because that was something *he* wanted. He just needed others to put an arm around him and say, "You can do this, Willie. We care about you, and we want to see you succeed." I realize that not everybody is in a position to help a person in the exact ways we were able to help Willie. But everybody is in a position to encourage and value a person who needs a second chance, the way Willie's co-workers at the hotel did. Willie felt like one of society's throwaways. I counted it a privilege to be one of many people who said, "No, Willie, you matter too."

# 6

# Digging Out

**O**ne of the biggest errors a businessperson can make is to treat fixed assets as if they were current assets. In my case, the long, slow process of getting out of trouble was a matter of undoing that mistake by converting fixed assets into current assets—and, more to the point, deciding to quit treating my business as ego fuel and re-focus on making money.

I don't gamble, but I do enjoy going to Las Vegas every now and then. It is an exciting place to watch the world. If you've ever been to a big casino, you've seen how things work in those gambling halls where hundreds of gamblers mill about—all of them thinking (wrongly) that the hotel was built by winners. No, those hotels are built by the losers. The house always wins.

At the craps table, people are standing four-deep as the dice are thrown, cheering as the man with the dice wins roll after roll. The gambler is on a roll, the numbers are coming up just so, and the crowd gets more and more into it. They place their bets, and they win alongside the man with the hot hand. But then everything goes quiet. The crowd disperses, the people wander off by ones and twos to find excitement in some other corner of the room. What happened? The man with the dice rolled craps. He lost. His winning streak is over, and now he stands alone. When you are on a roll, the crowd is right there with you, but when you roll craps, you will stand alone.

You see it all the time—not just in the casino, but in business and in life. The yes-men and the hangers-on disappear when the going gets rough. The winner has plenty of friends as long as he's winning. Once he starts to lose, he'd better watch out. Unless, that is, he has a developed strong inner resources and a strong support system of people whose trust he has earned.

When I played craps in the apartment business, I first thought I was the guy at the table. Lying there in bed, I imagined everybody wandering off to find some other winner to cheer for. But after a day or two of that kind of craziness, I began to understand everything that I still had. I thanked God for controlling those parts of my past that allowed me to still have the support of Marilyn and my children. They weren't going anywhere. I thought of everybody I had treated fairly, everybody for whom I had done a favor. Every good deed I had done was an asset—and I needed all of the assets I could get. I realized that I had banked a lot of good will. That good will was going to be the basis of my ability to get my financial house in order. And I realized something else: If I could pay off everything I owed—and I believed I could—I would be stronger than ever, both as a person and as a businessman. I had always thought it was success that would make my reputation. What if it turned out to be failure—or, more the point, a recovery from failure— that defined my reputation? I only focused on paying my bills; I didn't care if anything was left over.

My two days in bed were scary and I hope helpful in getting your attention as you read this book, but the truth is that we all find ourselves alone with ourselves in the dark every night.

How about you? When you lay your head on the pillow and you're struggling through a down period in your life, what is it that you think about? Who is the "you" that you're alone with? I hope you're able to think of all the people you've treated fairly and with respect. I hope you'll be able to answer yes when you ask yourself, "Do I like me?" If you can, you will find an inner strength that will move your attitude from fear of failure to hope for success. It's important to have friends who can reassure you that they respect and even like you. It is incredibly important to have that kind of confidence from within.

The truth is, you don't gather up those resources *after* the crisis has hit—or, in any case, it's a whole lot harder after the fact. The time to be banking that good will, those friendships and relationships, is when things are going well. When you have something to give—whether that's time, advice, money, encouragement—give it. The time may come when you don't have so much to give and will be relying on somebody else to help you out or show you some grace. The good news is that the things that really build your relationships and reputation are things that we all have access to: honesty, fair play, good faith, and good will. As much as we focus on capital and material resources in business, remember: those intangibles you have in your personal bank can't be taken away from you. They're incredibly important. Arrive at the point in your life where doing the right thing is second nature. Once you have asked God to help you make this transition, you will awake during a problem and realize that you have those assets in your bank. It worked for me.

You might want to stop reading for a minute and think about this "bank" that I've been talking about. What kind of deposits have you been making? When you need to make a withdrawal, are you going to have a positive balance? I'm not talking about rocket science here. I'm talking about treating people the way your parents taught you to treat people. There are real, tangible payoffs to being the person your parents taught you to be and the person you know God will be proud of.

---

In a previous chapter, I mentioned the danger of treating fixed assets as if they are current assets. I made the major mistake of looking at all the assets on my balance sheet as if they were the same. I had fixed assets—real estate, mostly—but without liquid assets, I was broke. Digging out of my deep, deep hole was mostly a matter of converting fixed assets into current assets until I was right side up again. In other words, selling properties to raise cash, using the cash to pay off creditors, and selling even more properties to raise more cash. All I had to do was to repeat that process until the *current* assets on the balance sheet were greater than the *current* liabilities. Sound easy? It wasn't—especially in the environment of the early- to mid-'70s. There was no more easy money and no booming economy to cover up all of the stupid things I had done. It would take five long years to pay back those hundreds of creditors.

I was walking a fine line between buying the time to sell real estate and keeping my creditors happy. I had one apartment project that I thought I could get two million dollars for—enough to pay off a sizeable number of my creditors. But you never know what something is worth until you sell, and that takes time. When you owe somebody $5,000, he's not impressed that you're waiting to sell a million-dollar property. He wants his money.

As I sold off properties, I needed fewer employees. Over five years, Jack P. DeBoer and Associates went from more than 2,000 employees to one single employee—me. But through it all, I was blessed to keep my family right side up and avoid bankruptcy and foreclosures. Those were years of serious soul-searching. I spent a lot of time redefining and reassessing what my personal skills really were. I thought I had lost the ability to develop real estate, and yet I didn't really know anything else.

Besides, I didn't have the cash to go into another business.

Most of the people in the field stayed with the properties as I sold them to others, but the changes in my corporate structure were very painful for me. I worked hard to find jobs for those people as I sold assets to others. I tried to cushion the blow by giving as much notice as possible and made no secret of the fact that the only solution was to downsize. Many came back to work with me as I rebuilt the business and have been with us for many years. They have positive things to say about how it all worked out. But it was painful. I worried more about them and their futures than I did about myself.

Through it all I was blessed to be able to keep my family right side up and avoid bankruptcy and foreclosures. Those were the years of serious soul-searching. I took a lot of time redefining and reassessing what my personal skills really were. I thought I had lost the ability to develop real estate, and yet I didn't really know anything else. Besides, I didn't have cash to go into another business.

Because I had taken the blame for my mess in the early '70s and hadn't tried to lie or cheat my way out of it, I still had the trust of people in my industry. So I was able to put together a deal to build the first Residence Inn. This idea was the beginning of the extended stay segment of the lodging industry—a new concept that now has more than 300,000 rooms in the lodging inventory. The year was 1975, the place, Wichita, Kansas. I hired a young decorator by the name of Kirstie Alley to do the interior design (yes, that Kirstie Alley). The extended stay segment of the lodging world has always had the best returns, and we had almost eight years building the Residence Inn system before anyone tried to copy us. I tell our teams not to worry about keeping secrets in the development business. Most people do not care what you are doing, and those who do care will find out anyway. So why waste the energy? I still own the original Residence Inn property, though it's no longer part of the Residence Inn chain. I changed the name to Cambridge

Suites. Recently, I completely remodeled the property, spending more than three times the original cost and repositioning it as The Hotel at WaterWalk.

One thing my business failures have taught me is to take the world's praise with a grain of salt. When you're successful, everybody around you tells you how great you are. That's nice, but in the end, it's a lot more helpful to look at your situation with a discerning eye. Think about how you got to the point where you are. What did you do right? What did you do wrong? And what was just luck? That's key. If you start taking credit for things that were just luck, if you mistake good fortune for good judgment, you're going to get yourself into trouble every time. Don't let it define your life and your personality.

In that spirit, I admit that I benefited from quite a bit of luck.

Sometimes ignorance is the mother of innovation. I didn't know anything about hotel chains. I knew about apartment buildings. So I didn't think of Residence Inn as a hotel, but as a short-term residence. And that, as it turns out, was just what the hotel business needed at that moment. It was definitely what this apartment developer needed. Apartment developers were getting hammered, not just by high interest rates and limited capital, but also by higher vacancy rates.

I was good at building apartment buildings in a cost-effective manner—certainly more cost-effective than the usual hotel construction project. So my brilliant (really just lucky) idea was to combine the construction costs of an apartment building with the lodging rates of a hotel. That suddenly made economic sense that neither apartment construction nor hotel construction was making at that time. I remember thinking that if we could get $17 per day for a suite, we would be in high cotton.

That first property was eight buildings with eight units each for a total of 64 suites. When I first envisioned the product, I called it "The Residence." And I was pretty serious about the idea of presenting it as a short-term residence rather than a hotel. I didn't want any hotel lingo in The Residence. We didn't use terms like "Front Desk," "Room Rate," "Guest Services," or "Check-in." The minimum stay was one month. Furnishings weren't included in the base rate. Borrowing the option up-selling model from car dealers, we offered detailed furnishing packages—so much for an alarm clock, for pots, pans, and dishes, for the bed, for linens. After all, none of those things are normally included in the rent when you rent an apartment.

We had a lot to learn. But the important thing was that we were willing to learn. We soon noticed that everybody who rented a suite also got the full furnishing package. So we got rid of the package model and just furnished every room. Our biggest customer at the time was Boeing. Boeing told us that they liked The Residence, but lots of their people didn't need to stay for a month. So soon we were renting by the week, and soon after that we were renting by the day. That made a huge difference in helping to make up the down occupancy on weekends.

The property was a success from the beginning, but we had a hard time explaining what exactly The Residence was. Was it a residence, or was it a hotel? The answer to that question would come, strangely enough, from Germany.

---

Twelve years earlier, in August of 1963, Marilyn and I heard a radio commercial placed by Youth for Understanding, the largest student exchange organization in the world. "Host an exchange student," the announcer said. So we did. Our son Sky was two years old and our daughter Penny was a new baby, but we accepted a German exchange student to live with us for a year. His name is Rolf Ruhfus. He was from Dortmund, a town in the Ruhr Valley along the Rhine River. With 800,000 inhabitants, it wasn't a small town, but few Americans had ever heard of it. Dortmund was about 90 percent destroyed by Allied bombing during World War II. Rolf's father, Irvin, was from a third-generation printing family and was an anti-aircraft gunner in Dortmund. Rolf was born while his mother, Lilo, was on the run from the war.

Rolf was 16 years old when he arrived to the U.S., and turned 17 shortly thereafter. He entered Portage High School as a senior and began a journey that was life changing for him, our family, and many others over years that followed. He became a full-fledged brother to Sky and Penny. Even though Marilyn and I are only 14 years older than Rolf, he has always called us Mom and Dad.

After graduating from Portage High, Rolf earned degrees from Western Michigan University, Wharton School of Business, and the University of Münster in Germany, from which he received a Ph.D. in marketing.

Life has a way of taking interesting turns. When young people ask me what I think they should do with their lives as it relates to business, I have a stock answer: Don't decide now, just get a broad education and keep your options open; doors will open and opportunities will come your way. The real challenge is making the right decision when those doors do open. In our case, it was a matter of paying attention to a radio ad and inviting a young German into our home. That small decision made a huge impact on people on both sides of the Atlantic Ocean. As it turned out, it also had a large impact on my professional life.

As Residence Inn began to prosper, I convinced Rolf to come back from Germany and join me in the business. It was one of the best things to ever happen to Residence Inn. Before Rolf joined us, we were proud of the fact that customers kept asking, "How can you do this for such a low price?" Rolf looked at us like we were crazy. He made us increase our rate until our customers stopped saying, "How can you do this for such a low price?" and started saying, "Yeah, that seems like a fair price." He moved the price per night from $20 to the $45 mark. I don't suppose you have to have a Ph.D. in marketing to realize that's a better way to price a hotel, but it certainly didn't hurt.

It was also Rolf who made me drop the whole "We're a residence, not a hotel" routine. He hadn't been there very long before The Residence became Residence Inn. And on the fence in front of each property we put a big banner reading, "YES, WE ARE A HOTEL." Not exactly subtle, but exactly what we needed. We had come a long way since being afraid to use hotel lingo.

We realized it was time we started thinking of ourselves as a full-fledged member of the hotel industry, not an apartment builder who happened to have built a few hotels. It wasn't long before we were true innovators in the business. We were first, for example, to offer free breakfast and to not do daily housekeeping unless it was requested. We found that our customers really liked not being bothered every day.

I remember the time I was talking to Jim Schorr, who was the president of Holiday Inn at the time. I asked him how much volume they were doing in food at their then 1,400 hotels. Almost a billion dollars, he told me. And they still lost money on food sales. We figured that in small hotels, it was cheaper to give food away than to sell it. We were right. Free breakfast became an industry standard. Once at an officer meeting at Residence Inn, the operations manager said he had a problem with supplying dishes in the units and free breakfast. It seems, he said, that they send their kids to the gatehouse with a plate to load up with donuts and bring them back to the room. "You mean," said the Vice President of Sales, "that the guests are eating the doughnuts?" Another lesson learned. We increased the number of doughnuts available.

When we had 16 hotels, we sold 80 percent of the Residence Inn brand (though not the real estate itself) to Brock Hotel Corp. from Topeka, Kansas. With the sale, we became a franchisee of Brock. They changed the name to Brock Residence Inn. We continued to build the properties while the folks in Topeka concentrated on selling franchises. It felt out of character, giving up that much ownership and control of a company we had built. But I was still stinging from the collapse of the apartment business and was in no mood to over-expand or otherwise expose myself to any more risk than was necessary. I hadn't forgotten the $100 million payout my ego had turned down in 1971. I had learned my lesson. This wasn't about ego or building the biggest chain anybody had ever seen. We were in business to make money, and the surest way to do that seemed to be to sell to Brock.

Risk only money. My new mantra.

Brock Hotel Corp., which was then a publicly traded company, began to focus on the pizza and entertainment business. Show Biz Pizza was expanding rapidly across the country, but business was slow. I knew what that felt like. I knew it was going to need lots of money. We saw our chance to buy back the 80 percent we had sold. I called Holiday Inn, and we put together a 50/50 joint venture to buy out Brock Hotel Corp.'s interest. The price was $20 million. We dropped the "Brock" and went back to the name "Residence Inn." We continued selling franchises and building our own hotels.

The business was very good. Residence Inn had grown to more than 100 properties when we decided to exercise the put-call provision of our Holiday Inn partnership. It was a simple "Abe Lincoln" arrangement, not very different from the routine where you tell one kid to divide the candy and the other to pick which piece he wants. We would name the price for a half-interest in the company, and Holiday Inn would decide whether to buy our half for that price, or sell their half to us for that price. It was a tough decision. If we set the price too high, we would end up overpaying for its half of the business. If we set it too low, Holiday Inn would own the entire business.

I traveled to Memphis and in a very short meeting with Mike Rose, Chairman of Holiday Inn, I nervously put a number for its half on the table: slightly more than $50 million. After what seemed to be several minutes of thought, Rose looked up at me and said that he was a seller and asked if I could come

Building the Residence Inn team, 1981.

Kathryn DeBoer, mother; Alfred DeBoer, father;
Jack and Paul DeBoer, brother, 1941.

**Above:** A new Second
Lieutenant, 1952.
**Left:** Senior at Michigan State
University, 1952.

DeBoer family in 1964: Marilyn, Jack, Skyler, German "son" Rolf Ruhfus and Penny, 1964.

**Above:** DeBoer family in 2004: Lynn DeBoer (who passed away suddenly in 2008), Skyler, Jack, Marilyn and Penny. Front: Christer and AJ.

**Above:** DeBoer family in 2011: Back L-R: Penny, Mimi Rogers, Annie and Christer. Front: Jack, Marilyn, AJ and Skyler.

**Above:** The first Residence Inn, 1971. **Below:** Reno, Nevada with Lyle Shelton and our winning unlimited race plane, 1986.

# The APARTMENT EMPIRE that JACK BUILT

Mobility, efficiency and flexibility have made Jack P. DeBoer Associates one of the nation's top 10 apartment builders and specialists in "over-looked" new markets.

Just as Wichita, Kansas, is near the center of America, Jack P. DeBoer is at the center of an unusually structured apartment development and management organization.

Abandoning the pyramidic corporate structure for a more functional team concept, DeBoer has taken a stylized, conservative apartment community into 14 of the Midwest's fastest growing apartment markets.

The apartment days, 1982.

**Above:** Young Company commander in the field, 1952.
**Below:** The joys of flying, 1998.

**Above:** We set the 3-kilometer world speed record this day. Wanda Odum and co-pilot Greg Tylski, 1995. **Top:** The company planes: Boeing 727, Cessna 208, Cessna 310, Learjet 35, North American SNJ 1942 and Cessna 172, 1990. **Below left:** The way to go, 1999.

The breakfast of adventure champions; for more than 50 years the "Ski Bums" have traveled the world's slopes. L-R: Jack, Ted Edison, Jack Swisher, Dick Greer, Joe Corsiglia, Kjell Vanghagen, John Bemis, Tom Wood and Don Prange.

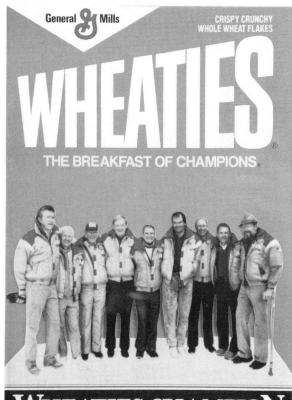

The experiences shared with friends could fill a book, but more importantly they filled my life. L-R Dick Greer, Jack, John Bemis, Kjell Vanghagen, Ted Edison, Jack Swisher and Tom Wood.

**Above:** Fun times with the Ski Bums: Back L-R: Kjell Vanghagen, Ted Edison, Jack, Tom Wood, Dick Greer, Jack Swisher and Don Prange. Front: Joe Corsigila and John Bemis. **Below:** Heliskiing took the Ski Bums off-trail in more ways than one. L-R: Jack Swisher, Tom Wood, Ted Edison, John Bemis, Dick Greer and Joe Corsigia.

2007.

**Above:** World Vision reports that our efforts over the past 20 years helped better the lives of 2.5 million Burmese people, 2009. **Below:** Our experiences in Burma transformed the way we think about the world and our place in it, 2009.

Our YPO Forum in Panama. L-R: Pack St. Clair, Jim Grier, JD Swanson, Jack, Frank Becker, Howard Brenneman, Fred Berry and Richard Felix, 2008.

University of Kansas Vickers Memorial Lecture, 2009.

Hotel Design: What's the Problem?

NOVEMBER 1998

A Penton Publication of
Development, Operations
and Marketing

LODGING HOSPITALITY

FLYING *the*
CONTRARIAN
FLAG

Lodging visionary
Jack DeBoer
gets a third wind
*with his*
Candlewood
brand.

The third hotel brand announcement, 1998.

Marilyn and I have been in step for every leg of our journey.
It's been quite a trip, 1984.

up with the money in two weeks. I was a little surprised; I had come into the meeting thinking he was probably be a buyer. So now where was I going to come up with $50 million in two weeks?

I called Rolf from the Holiday Inn limo on the way back to the airport. I told him the deal. Fourteen days to find $50 million to buy the other half of our company back. Rolf asked what I was thinking: deals of that size don't get done in two weeks. We considered all of our options and decided to talk to Marriott. We called John Dazburg, Marriott's President, and went to meet him in Bethesda, Maryland, the next day. We all understood that we weren't going to work out any actual deal— whether partnership or sale—in a mere two weeks. Instead, I asked John to loan us the money so we could close the deal with Holiday Inn. Then, if we could agree on a price for a sale to Marriott, fine. If not, we would repay the money over the next six months. It was clear that the value of the company was more than the sum of the two halves and that, with time, could get the money to repay Marriott. Of course, if we did not make a deal with Marriott or pay the money back, Holiday Inn would own the company for less than half its value.

As John can attest, he loaned the money to us in good faith, and we closed with Holiday Inn. Then we turned around and negotiated the deal to sell to Marriott. The folks at Holiday Inn always suspected we had a deal with Marriott before we had closed the deal with Holiday. But we didn't. People have often asked me why we sold to Marriott. We sold because Marriott thought Residence Inn was worth more than what we thought it was worth. As history has proven, Marriott was right. In terms of metrics such as highest returns and highest guest satisfaction, Residence Inn has been Marriott's best brand.

In a previous chapter, I had said that I was never an employee again after I got fired from my job as a soda jerk. That wasn't precisely true. When Marriott bought Residence Inn, I was officially an employee of the Marriott Corporation—from 8:00 one

Monday morning until lunchtime that same day, when I quit. I just didn't have it in me to work for somebody else.

When I arrived home at noon, Marilyn told me that she had married me for better or for worse, but not for lunch. My hanging around the house wasn't going to be an option. We had to have a plan for how we were going to spend our time. That is the subject of Chapter 9.

# The German Connection

Marilyn and I traveled to Germany and became close friends with Rolf's parents and many other wonderful German families. We have been back to Germany many times over the past 50 years. On one trip with my mother and our kids, we met the Schnorpfiel family in Tres Karden along the Mosel River. Heinz and Eda Schnorpfiel and five of their children have been our lifelong friends. Our kids have stayed with them and theirs have stayed with us. Heinz, while a member of the German army, walked home from the Russian Front as the Second World War ended and began processing stone on the family land. With little formal education, he built a successful company building roads and bridges with their own asphalt plants and stone quarries throughout southeastern Germany. Heinz is a typical German papa, seemingly in charge of everything. When his town needed a tennis facility, he built it and gave it to the city. The family owns apartments and supermarkets in several cities along the Mosel River. What Papa said was how it was.

Why do I tell you this? Because Heinz shows that part of being a strong leader is being able to hand over leadership to someone else. On his 65th birthday, Heinz walked into the corporate offices of the family business and told his eldest son Elmar, "I quit. You're in charge." He moved into a small office and began managing his other investments. I asked Heinz how he, who ran it all, could make such a decision. His answer was, "If it must be someday, why not now?" The company has prospered and grown even larger since that

*(continued)*

day. My father always told me, "The world should not be run by the withering hand of death." Heinz proved it.

CHAPTER 6: DIGGING OUT

# Stop Your Worrying!

Worry is the most unproductive activity in the world. A long time ago, long before I started paying attention to what my dad said, he told me, "Worry is something you can control very simply. Those things in life that you can do something about, do something about. Those things in life that you can't do anything about, forget about." Sounds easy. But does it work? Sure it does. It's a huge help to train yourself to recognize the difference between the things you can control and the things you can't.

Actually, there's one way that worry becomes productivity. If worry is a trigger that makes you get up and do something, then it's not all bad. If worry sends you into some kind of paralysis, that's not so good.

Here's a trick I use to deal with worry. When a problem comes up, I ask, "What's the worst thing that could possibly happen here?" Then, when I've answered that question, I ask, "Can I handle that?" The answer is almost always yes. Then I ask myself a third question: "Can I improve on that worst-case scenario?" It's a nice, positive approach to a problem. I get to work doing better than the worst-case scenario (which I've already decided I can survive if I have to). Anything better than the worst case is an improvement.

Another thing about worry: You have to learn to let go sometimes. We Americans all think we're Mr. Fix-It. When something happens we immediately think of how we can fix it so it will never happen again. It happens all the time in business. You need to train yourself to stop and think about what is really happening. Does

*(continued)*

it really need to be fixed? What happens if it just happens again? What energy will it take to fix it? Is the investment really worth fixing it? How much time will be wasted by others in getting it fixed? Is that a good use of their time?

Once you have answered the above questions, then you can begin to think about the solution. But not until you've answered these questions, or you will find yourself running around messing with unimportant issues.

# The Ski Bums

Life, in the end, isn't about money and things, but people. Marilyn and I have been blessed with many dear friends who have brought richness and joy into our lives.

More than 50 years ago, ten men in Kalamazoo, Michigan, formed a group to go skiing together the second week of February every year. We called ourselves SBOA, "Ski Bums of America." Nine of the ten men were either pilots or would become pilots. Every year since then, we have kept that promise to ski together. We have traveled to Europe and Africa, we have skied many areas in the U.S. and helicopter skied in British Columbia. We spent three days on the John C. Stennis, a nuclear aircraft carrier, during sea trials. Over the years, only twice did any of the group miss the outing. For a couple of years, the gathering was over a weekend, but soon it grew to a whole week. The Ski Bum group always wore matching jackets and hats. Our experiences would fill another book for sure.

Sometimes I told the group we were going to a secret destination. Once, we met at JFK airport in New York with ski equipment, and no one knew where we were headed. We boarded the overseas flight after it was ready to depart. The monitors at the gate were turned off. None of the group knew where we were going until they were in their seats on the airplane. The flight was bound for Morrocco and the Atlas Mountains. When we arrived in Casablanca, I was in great pain with a bad tooth. Doc Edison, a dentist and one of the bums, actually pulled the tooth in the wait-

*(continued)*

ing area of the terminal! The other bums stood around us in a close circle so other travelers wouldn't see.

Another time after a couple days of skiing in Aspen, I told the group we were taking another secret trip, and we loaded all the ski equipment on my airplane, closed the window shades, and departed. Everyone thought we were headed to Canada for more helicopter skiing, but after a couple hours in the air, I told the group to take off all of their clothes except their under shorts and watches. Seeing these old guys in the back of the Gulfstream in their underwear was a sight to see. We had purchased a complete wardrobe for everyone in the group, and a few hours later, we landed in Charlotte Amelie in the Virgin Islands to spend a few days on a private boat.

About 35 years ago, we had a serious discussion at dinner one evening. One of the bums said, "We have to consider that one of these times not all of us will be here." That summer, Lee Stryker was killed in his airplane. We agreed to never have a serious discussion again.

Can you imagine close friends honoring this kind of commitment for more than 50 years? Today, the group has aged. The Ski Bums of America are now down to six. Two of the six are no longer able to travel. We have so many memories that we share—and, as the SBOA draws to a close, there is much sadness that we share too; but even so, the important thing is that these memories are shared. Clearly another gift from a caring God.

# Beware the Man Who Always Worries About Being Cheated

Back in the '80s, I hired a man in Aspen, Colorado, to run and grow various companies I owned. I'll call him Gary. He was smart, handsome, and very articulate. Everyone liked him. He fit right in to the Aspen social scene and worked well with the county. I was confident that with Gary in charge, my money was well protected and all of our projects were moving ahead. He paid great attention to detail—especially when it came to making sure that nobody cheated us out of anything. At the time, I thought that was a good thing. After all, you can't be too careful, can you? Gary knew Aspen a lot better than I did, so it seemed good that he was always telling me who we should be wary of.

Whoops. I got that one wrong in a big way. One day my bookkeeper came to my office with a check written by our company to a vendor that had been deposited in to Gary's personal account. Then we noticed several loans that he had made to himself. The whole time he was warning me whom I should be watching out for—who was liable to cheat me—he was the one cheating me! I fired him that very day. He later got into a lending company with Aspen investors, and after a lot of their money went missing, he went to prison. When he got out of prison, he started a loan business in the southeast. Then, a few years ago, he committed suicide. A leopard doesn't change its spots, does it?

*(continued)*

I actually knew of Gary's troubled past before I hired him, but he convinced me that things weren't as they appeared and that it wasn't his fault. In retrospect, I know that his obsession with being cheated grew out of his own tendency to cheat.

I don't have the time or resources to always be covering my backside. I can't afford to give too much of my money to lawyers. Sure, I'd rather not get cheated. But we're all better off using our energies to keep moving forward, even if it means taking the occasional hit. Good people beget good people. The reverse is also true. Play it straight and honestly, and let the chips fall where they may.

My father always told me that you don't have to tell everything, but you sure as hell have to tell the truth.

# 7

# The Four Hotel Brands

*n the four hotel brands we started and operated, the model was to innovate (sometimes out of sheer ignorance of the norm) and then to adjust the formula, usually by slashing costs. One thing we've learned is to stay out of the middle: There's money to be made at the high end and the low end, but midscale hotels are a commodity—as is the case in so many industries—and there's little you can do to distinguish yourself. Your fortunes will, most likely, rise and fall with the economy.*

Over the past 30 years, we developed four lodging brands, all in the extended-stay segment: Residence Inn, which we sold to Marriott in the 1980s; Summerfield Suites, which is now owned by Hyatt; Candlewood, which we sold to InterContinental (Holiday Inn) in 2003; and Value Place, which we still own. Value Place is really not in the lodging business but rather in the short-term residential property business. It's positioned squarely between the apartment industry and the lodging industry for guests who can't afford lodging rates but don't want to commit to (or cannot afford) the leases required at apartments. True lodging (i.e., hotels) has an average length of stay between one and two days; apartments have a minimum stay of thirty days. With a minimum stay of seven days and an average length of stay of 10 weeks, Value Place—with 175 properties open to date—fills the gap with a low-price, clean, safe, and simple option.

I told the story of Residence Inn in a previous chapter. When I sold to Marriott, I signed a collared non-compete, which prevented us from opening hotels where the nightly rates would be between $55 and $75. We were free to go upscale or downscale from that middle range. My vote was to go downscale, but the rest of the team wanted to create a product with a higher price point. And so was born Summerfield Suites. The original concept was based on a two-bedroom suite with a kitchen and living room that could be occupied by two business travelers. It worked very well. The economics were favorable because the development cost of the second bedroom was much less than if it had been a freestanding single room.

Summerfield was an offering with rates near $100 per night. I felt that this higher price point limited the potential for growth. By the time we built 15 or 20 hotels—a good, solid beginning—I sold my interest in the company to Rolf and his partners in Germany. The chain remained small (even now it has fewer than 50 hotels). Eventually, the brand was sold to Hyatt. Rolf and his team moved on to even higher price points with their Avia brand.

Selling to Rolf and his team was not the most pleasant experience of my life. From the time we sold Residence Inn and signed the non-compete, we disagreed about the direction to take the company. I thought they had it all wrong when they tried to go upscale, and they thought I was wrong for wanting to go downscale. As it turns out, we were both right. As I have mentioned elsewhere in this book, staying out of the middle is a good strategy. They did fine with the higher-priced hotel, and I later demonstrated that a lower-priced option would work. It was the midscale segment that had become a commodity, with many viable options on most corners. Making money in the middle is difficult and tied mostly to the economy. All of the brands had basically the same offerings, and there was virtually nothing that anyone could do to separate itself from the pack. When the economy went down, the property went down. When the economy went up, the property went up. When you're selling a commodity, somebody else decides what price you can charge. Occupancy is shared among all the offerings and you have very little control over your share—maybe a couple of occupancy points for those who really do it better, but nothing of consequence.

By the time I sold my interest in Summerfield, the non-compete had expired and I was free to build a new midscale brand. I thought I had figured out how to make it work. I would reduce operating expenses. The average 100-plus suite Residence Inn had about 20 employees, as did all of the other midscale brands. An employee costs at least $25,000 per year. Applying a capitalization rate of ten, each employee reduces the value of a property by more than $250,000! So we went to work designing an operating model in which we could run a hotel with ten or 11 full-time employees. Shorter front desk hours was a major change; keeping the office open 24 hours required several extra employees. We devised a late check-in service that worked great and is still in use at all of the Candlewood hotels. We put small safes in the open area and told late check-in guests to look for the safe with their first name. They could punch in the first three letters of their last name, and the safe would open. There they would find a room key, a welcome note, and a quarter for their first drink from the Honor Cupboard. A Coke cost us a quarter, so that was all we charged in the Honor Cupboard. After all, we were in the lodging business, not the Coke business.

The idea of the Honor Cupboard was for guests to take what they wanted and leave a slip or put money in the slot. We didn't attend the Cupboard (another reduction in employee expenses!). We chose to trust our guests, believing that people are honest. The effort you spend trying to keep that less than one percent of folks from cheating you is much more costly than simply losing once in a while. When a person cheats you, after all, he's the one who goes to hell—not you. Besides, the prices were so cheap in the Honor Cupboard, it was hardly worth stealing. Did anybody ever steal a Coke from us? I'm sure they did. But there were plenty of people who just left a dollar in the slot and didn't worry about the change. Think about a mini-bar by contrast. When you're charging people four dollars for a can of Coke, they're motivated to figure out ways to steal that Coke from you. They can get pretty creative. And they don't feel very bad about it either. They feel that you're trying to steal from them by charging four dollars for something for which they're used to paying less than a dollar. You've started a game of measures and counter-measures—or, in any case, you've started a situation where there's not a lot of good will. I don't want to be in the business of making sure nobody's stealing soft drinks from me. That's not my core business. That gets too complicated too quickly. A quarter for a Coke—you'd be surprised how much good will comes out of a gesture as simple as that. By the way, after Intercontinental bought the brand from us, they raised the price to fifty cents. So they got, what, an extra few dollars per year? Was it worth it? I don't think so.

We paid close attention to our guests and what their needs were. Our guests were by and large business travelers. And in most locations, no more than ten percent of business travelers use a pool. So pools weren't part of the equation for Candlewood. We also learned that business travelers don't really care whether their hotel has a fancy lobby.

I already mentioned how we pioneered free breakfast at Residence Inn. Summerfield had free breakfast too, but when we started Candlewood, I thought about business travelers and what free breakfast meant to them. It meant getting up at least 30 minutes earlier and arriving when all of the newspapers were either gone or in great disarray, watching a TV program that someone else had selected, eating from paper plates, and sitting next to a stranger, all while eating cold, hard scrambled eggs.

Not the most pleasant experience in the world, but the guests still wanted breakfast at their hotel. The Candlewood Cupboard was our solution. All of the breakfast items were priced at or below our cost, and the guests picked up what they wanted the night before. In their full kitchen (every suite had one) they quickly prepared breakfast and ate it in their underwear. It worked. Candlewood is still the only national brand in the segment that does not give free breakfast. It enjoys occupancies at or slightly above the competition. Also, a Candlewood property operates with fewer full-time employees than its competitors.

Perhaps our biggest innovation with Candlewood was reduced housekeeping. Before we invented the extended-stay segment, the lodging industry treated every stay as if it was a series of one-day stays that required daily housekeeping. In the beginning at Residence Inn, we did what everybody else did, sending the housekeepers around every day. But if the turnover is weekly, why shouldn't housekeeping be weekly? When they're at home, people get by without daily housekeeping. Actually at Residence Inn, you have the option of daily housekeeping. Most weekends, people do not want to be bothered.

These huge savings made it possible to keep Candlewood in the middle range and yet provide great lodging spaces for our customers. Our suites were larger and better arranged, more user-friendly, with higher quality case goods and fabrics. Candlewood is still the best suite in that part of the industry.

All that to say, we did a great job on the operating model for Candlewood. We had low operating costs, the highest guest satisfaction in national surveys, high returns on investment, and high-quality construction (which saved us maintenance expenses and allowed us to capitalize the cost). Remember, it is much better to do it right the first time than to cheapen it and have to fix it later. It seemed to be paying off. In the startup months, we enjoyed double digit revenue growth every month.

So why, then, did we sell to InterContinental within just a few years of starting the brand?

We built and franchised 120 Candlewood hotels. That amount of hotels doesn't make for a recognizable brand, so we had to spend huge amounts of money on sales. We didn't do national advertising, so we focused on the sales side of things. We had more than 100 full-time Directors of Sales, each one costing more than $50,000 a year. We spent more than $12 million per year putting heads in the beds.

Marketing expense was a problem, but it wasn't the big problem. When we started construction on the first hotel, we borrowed $15 million from DoubleTree and started an active roll-out. In other words, from the get-go, we were growing faster than our current assets would allow. Then, in 1996, we took the company public. Everyone else was doing it. It seemed like a good idea. The company sold stock to several investment funds. Wall Street told us that growth was the key to stock growth. In the early days, they didn't care about profits. Sound familiar? I had supposedly learned my lesson about choosing growth over profits. That's what did me in back in the early '70s. The reason I was able to dig out was that I *quit* choosing growth over profits.

When we went public with Candlewood, I gave up a lot of my authority to steer the ship as I saw fit. All these new ship captains in a start-up public company wanted to know was, "How many sites do you have under contract? How many hotels do you have under construction? How many hotels do you have open?" It takes time to develop consistent profits, they said— which is true. But their willingness to put off profits until the future didn't sit well with me. We were actually making solid profits compared to other properties like us. But Wall Street said, "grow, grow, grow."

I should have seen what was happening—we were back to growth for growth's sake. The push was on. Business was good, revenue was growing and to get more capital, we sold nearly $500 million in hotels to a Real Estate Investment Trust. Then came March of 2001 and the beginning of another downturn in the economy, followed by 9-11. The leases had a fixed cost of 11 percent and there was no way out of them that in good times were below market. Business was slowing. Interest rates were falling rapidly, but we couldn't take advantage of the low rates. The stock had fallen far below the price at the IPO, and there was no way to access the public markets for additional capital.

Here is a lesson. Nowadays we do not have ANY debt that we cannot pay off anytime we wish. If you want to be open to the possible sale or major restructure of your company, keep your options in every possible corner of your business. If you have to negotiate a price in order to pay off debt early, do it. Remember, you have absolutely no control over the economy or interest rates. *Control what you can control.*

We had taken our eye off the basics of building a business in order to play the Wall Street game. Being public had an annual cost of millions of dollars. I could see the day when we would run out of cash. The development business is quite different than most other businesses. You go into and out of business every time you start and finish a development property. That's a big part of the reason the development business is so sensitive to changes in the economy.

We had a good operating company, good people, and a great product. But it was clear that we had to sell the company or run out of money. The board was made up of shareholders, all of whom, for the most part, had different agendas. Some held common stock, some held preferred stock, some wanted a short horizon and some a long horizon. The whole thing was pretty dysfunctional.

The REIT that held the title to almost all of the company hotels was willing to make some concessions to a buyer with a super strong balance sheet, but none to us. So we sold the company to InterContinental Hotel Group. A few months later, the hotel business began to turn around. Now InterContinental has a great brand that is growing nicely. See what happened? A company with plenty of *current assets* was able to ride things out and succeed. By going public, I got out from the worry of paying creditors. We were able to pay all our bills on time, and we never had a shortage of operating cash. Unlike creditors, shareholders roll the dice for what they hope will be higher returns. But at what cost? I may not have had debt to worry about, but I did have to worry about stock price, and that was something I had little control over.

What did I learn?

Growth for the sake of growth is a recipe for failure.

Giving up financial flexibility is stupid. We could not get out of the leases.

Internal pressures divide and external pressures unite. We had lots of internal pressures within the top leadership in the company that I simply did not fix. In retrospect, I could have fixed it by changing the players, but I did not.

Look carefully at your reasons for going public. It will change the way you view your business and, unfortunately, how you must run your business. Most of the time, equity capital is the most expensive of all capital sources. Small public companies spend way too much money just being public. Chasing the stock dream can be fun, but don't risk the farm.

Competing in a business that has become a commodity does not reward the players who do things just a little better. When all of your competition is doing a good job, you will be driven by external forces. When the business is good, everyone enjoys it. When it is bad, everyone suffers. In that arena, financial flexibility is absolutely critical.

I am an entrepreneur. Entrepreneurs do not function well in

structured environments. When the entrepreneur is the strongest personality and the business has become management intensive, watch out.

The good news is that Candlewood was able to fulfill all of its obligations to other businesses and to its employees. The only financial pain came to those who made bets for high returns—*i.e.*, stockholders. Including, of course, me.

So yes, I did experience some pain when I decided we needed to sell Candlewood. But it wasn't the kind of excruciating pain I experienced in 1971. I was in a position to bounce right back, and I felt I knew exactly how to do it. Our fourth brand would be Value Place.

I had tried midscale extended-stay hotels, and I had tried upper-midscale. But I was convinced that downscale was the best way to go, especially after the operational wisdom I gained from Candlewood. As I have said, in the lodging business, the middle range is a commodity, like wheat or sugar. If you want to know how much your sugar is worth, just look on the Internet. But you can't make your sugar any sweeter. The lodging products in the middle have good, well-run competition on most every street corner in this country. All of these hotels are pretty clean, they're run pretty well, and they're priced about the same as the one on the adjacent corner. Consumers choose a hotel mostly on price or the point credits they enjoy with the major brands. You can have a better front desk, a pool, offer breakfast, and have nicer landscaping, but you will rise and fall with the market. When business is great, you and your colleagues will think you are really smart. When the economy or local problems take business away, you will feel dumb. The worst part is that you cannot do anything meaningful about it.

How does this apply to your business? All industries are segmented. The challenge is to pick the right segment in your industry—the segment where you can have the most effect on your business by *your* actions, not those of the market or others on the outside.

So why Value Place? In Value Place we live by four rules:

- Lowest Price.
- Cleanest.
- Safest.
- Simplest.

In terms of operating costs, Candlewood was a huge improvement over Residence Inn. But we knew we could slash costs even further, and that was going to be the key to success in our new endeavor. As I mentioned, we were spending $12 to $14 million a year on Directors of Sales at Candlewood. That, at that time and place, probably was a wise investment; it was a lot more focused and a better sales tool than mass media, for instance. We had a good sales force that managed to compete very effectively with chain brands that had the benefit of better name recognition. But as we began to envision our new brand, we wondered what it might look like *not* to have a Director of Sales at every location. In the midrange, a Director of Sales was vital; we were selling a commodity, so we needed somebody to make our case. But if we could get the price way down without sacrificing cleanliness, safety, or comfort, we might not need sales directors. And not having sales directors and other staff would help us get the price way down. It was a positive cycle. The key would be to get the price down and then make sure our customers were aware of the price.

So how would we create awareness of a startup brand without the resources to do a major marketing program? Our answer was electronic signs. Electronic signs show up for work every day, 24-7, and send a consistent message to everybody who passes by. Value Place now has almost two hundred electronic signs seen by more than 50 million drivers every day. We know they work because almost half the people staying in Value Place say they are there because they saw the sign. Those signs alone represent more than $12 million per year in savings.

Then there was the staffing. We were pretty proud of our operating model at Candlewood, which took us from an average of 17 to 20 full-time employees at Residence Inn to ten to 12. We examined our operations and discovered that we could run a clean, safe, comfortable property with four and a half full-time employees. Those were huge savings. On top of the marketing and staffing savings, we designed a building that could be delivered for less cost per square foot. Those two things gave us a huge price advantage.

We focused on providing only those things that every person staying with us would use. No pools, no breakfast, no meeting rooms, no gyms, no daily housekeeping. That makes it possible to provide a very low price which, in turn, means high occupancy. If our average weekly rate is $200, that's less than $30 per day. Are those things we're missing worth $75 a day to the average long-term business traveler? I don't think so.

In any business, need plus awareness equals the ability to compete. In other words, when you've identified a need and made the world aware that you're able to meet that need, you're in a position to compete with others. Our goal was to change the formula. With Value Place, we wanted the formula to read, "Need Plus Awareness Equals WIN." We identified the need at its most fundamental: What do extended-stay lodgers *really* need, and what are those extras that simply don't matter? By zeroing in on actual and not imagined needs, we found huge savings in both construction and operations. Those savings were so huge, in fact, that once we made people aware, we had won. We didn't need a sales force. Need Plus Awareness didn't just equal the opportunity to compete. Need Plus Awareness equaled a WIN. Value Place was born.

In a very short time, Value Place had become the fastest-growing housing brand in history. Value Place is the home run of all our brands. I am often asked if I have another brand in me and I smile and shrug and say, "Who knows?"

Simplicity. I keep coming back to it because I keep coming back to it in my business life. Where I have enjoyed success, it has been because I kept things simple. I'm not saying that life or business are by nature simple. I'm saying that because it's *not* simple, you have to simplify that which can be simplified. You need a few simple rules that can control the many choices you have to make in a complex environment.

Value Place is a great example. It's all about price, cleanliness, safety, and simplicity. Any time we make a decision at Value Place, we ask ourselves what would further those four goals. Like the Honor Pantry at Candlewood, we kept it simple: *Here are some snacks. We hope you'll pay the very nominal price we're asking. But we're not going to complicate things by making sure you don't steal from us.* If our core business was snacks, we might not have been able to take that approach. But our core business was running a clean, safe, comfortable hotel. We kept it simple.

Of all the simplifying rules in the world, perhaps the most helpful is the one we call the Golden Rule. Treat others the way you would want to be treated. Treat customers the way you want to be treated. Treat employees the way you want to be treated. Treat vendors the way you want to be treated. Even treat competitors the way you want to be treated. I don't expect my competitors to stop competing. I just expect them to compete fairly and honestly. So that's the way I compete. We spend no time or money keeping secrets from our competition. Most don't care to copy us. Those who do try to copy us inevitably tinker with the formula. And the formula simply doesn't need to be tinkered with.

Every time I speak to a group of employees, I talk about the Golden Rule. It's a key part of the culture of any company I'm a part of. If you want to get the most out of your employees, you have to care about their well being. I've said a lot in this chapter about cutting costs, but cutting costs doesn't mean shafting your employees. There are a lot of unskilled and semi-skilled positions in the lodging industry. That means we have a lot of employees who haven't had an easy go of it. All the more reason to take care of our employees.

Culture is set by leaders' actions, not by directives or rules. Nobody in any of our companies wonders if "treating people the way you want to be treated" is the way we do business. I set the example by modeling the behavior I expect from my employees. I don't ask them to be more considerate, honest, or hard working than I am. Actually, our people think I am a soft touch; I'm okay with that. We try to be fair but tough; though, admittedly, most of the toughness comes from my managers, not from me. You'll never have to tell your employees how to treat their customers if you model (and remind them of) the Golden Rule: Treat others the way you would like to be treated.

When we still owned Candlewood, I got one of the most touching birthday presents I ever received. The team members at each of the properties got together and had their pictures taken—many of them with their families. They then compiled all of the photos into a book that they gave me on my birthday. As I paged through the book, I was struck by how few white faces there were. Our employees in the field were overwhelmingly Hispanic, Asian, and black. As I looked into their faces, it occurred to me that I didn't really know what their lives were like. So I decided to find out. We started asking questions. "What is the biggest problem you're dealing with in your life?" "How can we make your life better?" We were talking about their lives, not their jobs.

The results were amazing. The number-one problem that our employees dealt with was childcare; it's not cheap. The second-most common problem was keeping a car running. I am glad we asked. It had been many years since I'd had real car trouble I would have never guessed it. The third problem was an inability to communicate with the home office in Wichita, where our people only spoke English. In other words, if a Spanish-speaking employee had a problem with his or her boss, there was no good way to tell the boss's boss. (By the way, if you are a manager in any of our companies, you put your job at risk if you prevent your employees from going over your head.)

As a result of that research, we started a program called "We Care." We negotiated with daycare businesses in various cities to give our employees a lower rate. We wondered how a car dealer might deal with our employees if a manager accompanied them to negotiate the deal—even if the manager didn't say a word. It was clear that a better deal would be offered. We identified local car dealers whom our employees could trust—dealers who knew they would get more business from us if they treated our people well, and that they would lose our business if our employees complained. In the home office, we put together a team of people with language skills to help our employees whose English wasn't strong. We entered into a business arrangement with Market Place Ministries, a national organization that makes pastors available to employees who may have personal issues in their lives. I was amazed at how much resistance I received from some of the senior officers in the company. In this instance, we did not count the votes; we weighed them. As a result, we implemented "We Care." It affected lives positively. And I am absolutely certain that it paid for itself in spades.

Those efforts made a huge difference for our employees. There are plenty of good reasons to take care of one's employees, some moral, some more pragmatic. From a business perspective, it makes a huge difference in recruiting and retention.

I have found the Golden Rule to be as important on the franchise side of things as on the employee side of things. We have built four successful franchised brands, and I still haven't read a franchise agreement or the UFOC (uniform offering circular). I let the team that runs franchising deal with that. All that legal mumbo-jumbo comes down to protecting people from other people who don't behave decently—who don't treat others the way they would want to be treated. I'm not saying franchise agreements or UFOCs are unnecessary. Unfortunately, they sometimes are. We live in a world where some people ignore the Golden Rule, and where people will sue other people at the drop of a hat.

Fortunately, those folks are in the minority. If they were not, then democracy as we know it simply would not work. When we find ourselves in business with folks who do not play by what is right and fair, and it happens, we move quickly to separate ourselves from them. Life is much too short, and the money is not worth being in a business relationship without mutual trust. This has nothing to do with being "holier than thou." It has to do with YOU and who you are and who you associate with. I promise those relationships will take away from the real reason to be in business. We have discussed that. You must not operate in a business relationship that is less than fair and honest, or it will change who you are. And besides, it is not fun.

Having said all of that, however, I will say that we have never been sued by a franchisee, nor have we ever sued a franchisee, and there is a very good reason. Our philosophy is that there are three things that make a franchise system work, and none of those three things are found in the franchise agreement or the UFOC. The three things that make a franchise work are:

1. The franchisee makes money.
2. The franchisee makes money.
3. The franchisee makes money.

That's all that matters in a franchise. Everything else is secondary. This philosophy has certainly worked for us. It puts everyone in the same boat working on a common goal. We have never added a fee to services provided to the franchisees, and we never will. It clouds whose side people are on. We've never been sued because when problems happen, and they do, we work out the best solution for everyone involved. Providing whatever is required for the franchisee to be successful is what makes a franchise work. We do it.

The good news is that over the years, many of our franchisees have become independently wealthy. Of that I am very proud.

# Assessing a Franchise

Many franchise companies begin because of greed on the part of the franchisor. An entrepreneur with a couple successful stores pulls out a clean yellow sheet of paper and, without considering exactly why the original stores are succeeding, he multiplies how much money he can make by selling his idea to lots of other businesspeople. Franchise fees, royalties—it sounds like a great business. The power of the brand will make the numbers grow for everyone and profits will not be far behind.

But things on the franchisor's side often look a lot different from things on the franchisee's end. Selling franchises to others is clearly a smaller risk than running the business yourself. Franchise royalties are paid off the top line; every business has some top line. Before you invest in a franchise, ask yourself how much money and how many businesses the franchisor has at risk.

When franchises fail, it's often because they were ill prepared, or the basic business model is flawed or too complex for the average businessperson to execute. Ask yourself: Is this model easily translated? Franchise law is complex and forces the franchiser to jump through hoops and disclosures to see what is happening to the businesses already in place. But still, lots of people who buy franchises lose a lot of money. Why? The human brain digests good news easily; it is more difficult to focus on potential bad news. Even worse, a human looks at how another is doing and is convinced that he can do better. Be careful: Look hard at the basic business before you invest. Also, consider that franchise

*(continued)*

law restricts what the franchisor can tell you about the actual financial results you may expect. Talk to franchisees who are operating businesses in the system. They can tell you straight. Ask the franchisor for names and contact information so you can make those calls.

So, if most franchises fail or never grow to reach any meaningful size, how are some successful? When the business model works and is supported by brand growth, then you have the basics for success. Analysis of a franchise is pretty easy. You only need to answer a few questions:

1. Does the basic business model work? I mean, does it make money?
2. Will awareness among potential customers make the business do better? In other words, is there brand value?
3. Who is behind the franchisor? Will they keep the standards of the system intact as it grows?
4. Are you willing to put in the time, effort and money to make your business work?

Pretty simple I would say.

In every brand we founded—Residence Inn, Summerfield Suites, Candlewood Suites, and Value Place—we owned more properties than our franchisees for the first few years, and we continued to build properties ourselves. We always listened to the franchisees because none of us is smarter than all of us.

# Control Your Company's Destiny

We sold Candlewood Suites because we lost the right to do what we considered best for the company. Over-expansion, serious miscalculations by our financial team and me, and a slump in the lodging industry took away the cash flows that had hidden our dumb mistakes. I pushed to sell in a down market because we were burning cash at the operating level and trapped in leases that demanded 11 percent in a debt market that demanded five percent. We sold nearly all of our hotel properties to Hospitality Properties Trust. When the market was expanding, everything was rosy; all the potential upside stayed with our company. But the downside in a contracting market is disastrous. We couldn't pre-pay leases that were killing us. We gave up control in two different ways that turned out to be a double whammy. We over-expanded (against my better judgment) at the insistence of Wall Street, and we financed that over-expansion with debt that couldn't be paid off at a time that was best for the company.

Why do I even bring this up? It is great lesson on picking the ground on which you want to fight. It is important that your business is aligned with players who have the same goals. In a public company, you will be judged on how you did during the last 90 days. In a start-up public development company, we were first graded by how many sites for hotels we had under contract, then by how many starts we had, then by how many were open. The game was to drive the stock higher in order to leverage the stock to raise more capital to build more hotels, which would then raise

*(continued)*

the stock even higher to gain even more leverage to raise even more capital to build even more hotels—an upward spiral. To my knowledge, there has never been a public hotel start-up that succeeded in the long run. I knew it then, but I refused to believe it. There were some start-up public hotel companies that were success- ful for the shareholders if they SOLD soon enough, or if the sponsors bought more stock when it was down and then sold the company. If I had done my home- work, I would have known this and sold within the first two or three years.

# The Dangers of Going Public

As I've mentioned several times, you're either an entrepreneur or a manager. I'm a good entrepreneur and a lousy manager. Entrepreneurs and public companies are like oil and water. I failed at running a public company, and I learned a few lessons along the way that are worth repeating.

Far be it from me to opine on going public except to say this: Don't be seduced by the lure of easy money. In the private arena, making cash profits is the simple formula for success. In public companies, success comes from many corners and often success or failure has nothing to do with how you run the business. There are people for whom that works out just fine. For me, it was a terrible setup. I needed to be in a business where future success would be achieved by my actions, not forces over which I had limited or no control. Being public changes the focus of business to short-term thinking. You have to succeed every 90 days to keep your stock from falling in value. It has a way of destroying much of the strategic planning that is so important in all businesses.

I would also point out that being public is really hard on a small company. All the mandatory public reporting takes almost as long for a small company as it does for a large company. Which means, as a percentage, you're spending a lot of your time on that stuff that has no direct bearing on the success of your company. On top of that, I believe there's such thing as too much money too early. Too little money tends to sharpen a businessperson's skills and heighten his

*(continued)*

problem-solving abilities. Too much money sounds like a good problem to have, but it actually does take a special kind of manager to strike a balance between growth and good sense.

# 8

# Choices and Simplicity

The world is a complex place. In a free society, you are constantly called upon to make choices, and those choices have real consequences. So how do you make those choices and make them well? By simplifying. By reducing a whole world of choices and gray areas to black-and-white questions you can act on. That simplification principle applies to everything from hiring to using your Blackberry to simply being who you are.

A great deal of the successes in my businesses came from sticking with what I know best. The majority of my earnings came from the development and lodging industries. I learned those businesses inside and out, and it served me well. But I have also been involved in dozens of side businesses. And most of them, as I have said before, failed.

When I say they failed, I don't mean they went bankrupt or that we didn't pay our creditors. They didn't make money, so we closed them down—and knowing when to cut your losses and stop throwing good money after bad is one of the most important business skills a person can have.

More than once, I have referred to the entrepreneurial mindset—that optimistic thinking causes a person to see the upside of an opportunity more clearly than the downside. Boy, do I have a bad case of it. I can't help swinging for the fences. And when you swing for the fences, you're bound to strike out a lot. On balance, my businesses outside of the core development and hotel businesses were profitable. A bunch of failures were covered by a few real wins. I guess you'd call that luck.

I see it over and over again with my friends (just as I've seen it with myself). An entrepreneur makes a lot of money in his own business, and then he loses a lot of it by investing in somebody else's business. Why? Because when you look at someone else's business from the outside, you tend to know all of the good stuff before you make the investment. You find out all of the bad stuff *after* you make the investment.

And yet I still invest in outside companies. I don't do it because I'm a glutton for punishment; I do it because I think I've discovered the exception to the rule. I don't invest in businesses; I invest in *people.* My investment dollars go with people whom I believe to be talented and honest—people I expect to win. And I have learned (better late than never) to leave those people alone and let them run the business.

The best example of this is my partner, Bruce Heulat. If you've read this far, you know that I love airplanes. I love them so much, in fact, that I sometimes assume I know all there is to know about the aerospace industry. So when a couple of aircraft engineers approached me in the '80s and asked if I wanted to be a part of a kit airplane manufacturing company called Prescott Aviation, I said, "Sure." It sounded like a fun, fantastic opportunity. Kit planes are great. Who wouldn't want one? I hadn't been in the business long when Duane Wallace, Chairman of Cessna Aircraft, sat me down and told me to get out of the business as soon as possible. I had enormous respect for Duane, but what did he know? Sure, he started the Cessna Aircraft Corporation with a hope, a dream, and some seed money he had won on the airplane racing circuit, and then built it into one of the most important aviation companies in the world. But I was a pretty smart cookie myself. I had built a lot of apartments and hotels.

The whole thing went downhill fast. Duane Wallace had warned me that the kit industry was historically awful; history definitely repeated itself with Prescott Aviation. On top of that, the guys running the company had no business running a company. The business was hemorrhaging cash.

Meanwhile, Bruce Heulat, who had been running a manufacturing company owned by Wichita's Koch Industries (the second-largest private company in America), found himself out of a job when Koch sold the company. I knew Bruce by reputation, so I hired him on the spot to straighten out Prescott Aviation. His first day of work was a Thursday. The next Sunday he showed up at my door and told me the company was a bottomless pit and I should get out as soon as possible.

That made a huge impression on me. Bruce wasn't interested in keeping his job; he was interested in doing the right thing. I told him to do whatever needed to be done to fill all of our commitments to the people building the Prescott Pusher, then to close the company down. When that was done, I told him he should go out and find a viable manufacturing business for sale. I would put up the money, and he would run it and have a 25 percent ownership interest. A few months later, we bought Hix Corporation in Pittsburg, Kansas. At that time, the company manufactured machines for the clothing imprint industry. In the last 20 years, Bruce has expanded the business to many other projects with almost no management input from me. Today he is a multimillionaire, and I have made back my Prescott loss a few times over. I still don't know anything about the manufacturing business.

So what is the lesson here?

The best investments I've made have been investing in people like Bruce who do the right thing and have the ability to be successful. With people like that, you know that even a failure isn't a disaster. Hix Manufacturing makes, among other equipment, the majority of the world's heat transfer machines. Once computers were able to scan a photo and create a transfer to be applied to a garment, Bruce and I thought putting personal photos on T-shirts would be a great business. We formed Express Designs and opened up inside grocery stores and malls. We began franchising and thought we had a real winner. Why shouldn't it have been? The world wears T-shirts, and this technology was new and exciting. The people who ran the business were good folks who worked hard. I just knew it was going to be a great business. The stores actually made some money, but the company itself never made a profit. We kept throwing good money after bad, convinced that we would make a profit once we got sales up. Several million dollars later, we closed the business.

What is the lesson here? Even if you have good people running a business, it may not *be* a good business. Closing a business is much harder than opening one. Knowing when to fold is more important than knowing when to bet.

Outside of my core businesses, the businesses in which I weren't closely involved were the ones that made the most money. That is a sobering thought. But the lesson is simple once again. Stick to what you know, and when you venture out, spend more energy deciding who your partners or employees are going to be rather than on the business itself. There are always exceptions; I had a business or two that made some money in spite of the fact that the partners wouldn't pass muster for me today.

But Bruce was a treasure, and, as a consummate manager, he was a perfect complement for an entrepreneurial dreamer like me. He's the guy who breaks the bad news and brings me back to Earth, balancing out my runaway optimism. And he throws nickels around like manhole covers. Because I have left him alone all these years, the business has thrived and is a healthy profitable business today.

I've seen a lot of business schools that match up mentoring relationships between business leaders and folks who are starting businesses. It's a great concept and will help startups succeed. As I thought about what they were doing, it occurred to me that putting entrepreneurs with entrepreneurs would be a recipe for disaster. Together they would make each other feel wonderful and lay out an exciting business plan in whatever business the young entrepreneur was starting. And that business would probably be doomed too early. Entrepreneurs need managers as mentors and managers need entrepreneurs as mentors.

---

Life and business are about choices—choosing partners, choosing when to bet, choosing when to fold. And choice requires action. The desire to achieve is one thing, but it must be coupled with strong determination if it's going to result in anything. People with lots of energy think about doing all kinds of creative things. But without the strong determination to get something done, the dreams simply pass away without action. Dreaming up a plan is one thing, but it is important to have the ability to set the plan into motion and follow it through to its conclusion. The conclusion could be, "This is crazy; it can't possibly work." That understanding is just as important as, "Wow, this is better than I thought." The old phrase, "don't send good money after bad," applies to many areas of life: the direction of energy, pursuit of love, sticking with a bad business decision, or maintaining a bad health habit.

Life is a continuing series of choices. That is the price we pay for living in a free society. Achieving a full, happy, successful, meaningful life is simply a matter of making better choices. Your choices begin when you awake in the morning and don't end until you fall asleep at night. Choices build on each other; a bad choice will often force you to continue making bad choices.

Think about smoking, drinking, drugs, laziness, bad attitude, obesity, lack of education, and so on. Things work out a whole lot better if you never smoke the first cigarette or drink the first drink, if you never start overeating or drop out of school. Reversing a series of bad choices is a lot more difficult that simply not heading down the path.

In the same way, choices in business also build on each other. The first time you write a check without money to cover it makes doing it the second and third times much easier, until finally you hit the wall. Little bad choices lead to big bad choices that start you down the road to a ruined life. Think about the latest business executives to go to jail. I'm thinking again about the guys from Enron, Global Crossing, and MCI, but by the time you read this there will probably have been others that are fresher in your memory. Do you think those guys skipped straight to investor fraud and insider trading? No, they all started down the road to ruin with a few small, bad choices. No one is born dishonest. Dishonesty is learned, and it is honed with practice. It builds as the result of getting away with just a few simple lies. Every liar knows he's a liar. And he won't be proud of it. So as I have said before, when you wake in the morning, start your days by asking yourself that simple question: "Do I like me?" If you can honestly answer yes to that question, you are on your way to success and happiness.

It clarifies things to think of life as a series of choices. But it can also be daunting. There are a lot of choices. And they all matter. How on Earth do you make sure you're making the right choices when they never end? If you've ever run a business or a household, you know how the decisions come at you one after another. They simply don't stop. Actually, "one after the other" isn't accurate. That would be relatively easy. Unless you're a hermit or a child, choices come all at the same time. And most of them are important.

Once again, I have found that my most important key to success has been keeping my basic business simple. I know the principle of simplification sounds funny coming from a guy who always keeps as many plates spinning as I do. But if I wasn't actively searching ways to keep my decision-making process focused on the basics, I could never keep the plates spinning. This is a complex world we live in. Each of us only has control over a very small piece of it. That's why it's so important to pay attention to that tiny sliver we can control, and keep the choices within that little sliver as simple and straightforward as possible. Boil things down to their essence, make a decision, and then act on your decision. If things are gray, make them black and white. I know, I know; you can miss some nuance when you make everything black and white. It's a chance I'm willing to take. And when it comes to personal relationships, you should probably allow for some gray. But in business, don't be afraid of the black and white.

By producing actionable decisions, black-and-white thinking can set you free from worry and dithering. The only remedy for worry is to take action to address whatever is worrying you. To sit there paralyzed by worry doesn't do you one bit of good. Worry on one hand and spit in the other. Which hand do you think will fill up faster?

## Monkeys

When I was running the apartment company, I was an attentive micro-manager. I had the reputation of being a nice guy to work for, and I tried very hard to follow the "treat others as you would like to be treated" rule. To build on that rule, when someone asked me to do something, I thought I had to do it. WRONG. The Golden Rule has nothing to do with doing everything that is asked of you.

Everyone travels through life with a bunch of monkeys. Monkeys sit on your head, hang on your belt, live in your pockets, brief case, and telephone; they're absolutely everywhere. The name of the game in business is to only take the monkeys you can feed. Starving monkeys smell, and they ruin your reputation.

In the old days, when I was headed down the hall going to a meeting, someone coming from the other way would say, "Jack, I need to talk to you about the deal in Denver." My response was always, "That's important and I really want to discuss it with you. *I will call you.*" Zap! That guy's monkey jumped off of him and onto me. It made me a nice guy and it satisfied the other guy, but soon I had starving monkeys. Monkeys travel through cell phones, faxes, FedEx packages, and the Internet. They run wild in all kinds of meetings and are always looking for someone to feed them. Let's replay the meeting in the hallway with the new Jack. "Jack, I need to talk to you about the deal in Denver." The monkey is ready to jump. Now I say, "The Denver deal is important and I want to discuss it with you. I am headed for a meeting but will be in the office this afternoon. *Please call me.*" Keep your own damn monkey.

It is important that you take the monkeys you can feed and feed them well. That's how you get ahead as you travel through your business life. In meetings when the monkeys are running all over, pick the ones that are important to the task at hand and the ones you know need a champion. And do not leave the meeting, if you are running it, without finding a home for all of the wild monkeys in the room.

## Technology and You

When I walk through the office on my howdy rounds each day, I am aware that we do not have a single machine or device that my father had in his real estate and insurance business. No typewriters, no phones with lighted push buttons, no carbon paper, no intercom boxes, no switchboard receptionist, no Dictaphone machines, no ink pens or ink wells, no adding machines, no gum erasers, no 35-millimeter slide projectors, no men's hats on the rack, no white shirts and ties, no PA announcements of arriving phone calls. How does this affect the way we work and the way we live our lives?

As each change came along over the years, I adapted and, slowly but surely, it changed the entire way I work and think. Junk mail was elevated as fax machines and e-mail replaced special delivery mail. Phone calls can be taken from anywhere, at home or while driving. A fax machine found its way into my home, followed by a computer, so that I could stay in touch by e-mail at all times. When the laptop allowed my business world to follow me on the road, I wondered if it was all that good. The final straw was the Blackberry. All of the executives in our company got them, and they gave me one as well. I had it on my belt for a week before I realized that 99 percent of whatever came over the dumb thing was stuff that either was not important or could be handled at a later time. I returned it and also turned off my cell phone for a week or so. It was like a vacation. I doubt if the people who are always looking at them in meetings really need the information at that moment. Checking your Blackberry in meetings is impolite and distracting.

Most gadgetry allows you to keep up with every little unimportant thing in your life at lightning speed. Is that good? It makes you stop real planning because you know that at any time you can fill in the blanks with an email or a phone call. People are addicted to instant response and instant knowledge to the point where they have absolutely no time to use their brains for what is really important. Take a look at all the stuff you get at instant speed—do you really need to know it at that time? Is it that important? I doubt it. What ever happened to just letting the world know where you are so you can be contacted in an emergency? Or, more importantly, taking control of your life and being proactive?

I now call my secretary a couple of times a day to check in. If you do not have a secretary, turn off your Blackberry and your cell phone until you see what is going on. The first thing you will notice is that the number of e-mails and phone calls you get will be reduced significantly. If I were King, I would make it a rule that no computers have the ability to store group addresses that allow messages to be sent to multiple people with one click of the key. Instead, it would be necessary to type in each address that you want to reach. This would eliminate at least 75 percent of all the e-mails you get, most of which are important for others but not for you. It would save hundreds of hours of wasted time for the people who have to read stuff that is not important to them.

That's not to say that you can just dispense of your cell phone. And email, when managed, can be a help. My dad used to tell me that I should keep track of my calls. If I received more calls than I was placing, I was not in control of my world. The same is true of your cell phone. Shut it off when you want to use your mind for something useful and pick up your voicemails when it is convenient. Granted, when you are involved in something *really* important, you should be available on your cell phone. But how often does that happen? Perhaps guarding your cell phone number is a good plan. Is the number of e-mails you receive a day a badge of how important you are? People delight in telling me how many emails they get. Nuts. Tell me how much you got done.

The cell phone and the Blackberry are very important for some people. You can figure out who they are: salesmen, doctors on call, etc. Most people, however, have been caught up in the instant syndrome. It dulls your brain and steals important time from you.

The point of all of this is to stress the importance of using your brain time as well as your clock time for important issues, and not just keeping up with all the stuff flying around in space that lands in your cell phone, laptop, or Blackberry.

People who do piece work and put in more hours doing the task they get paid for can probably justify longer hours - but can you? How much of your day is spent doing things you will never get paid for? Are you just trying to convince others how hard you work? Are you really using your time on things that matter

CHAPTER 8: CHOICES AND SIMPLICITY

to your success? Effective use of time is the key to success, not long hours.

Do I have a cell phone? Yes. Does my card have the number on it? No. Do I have a computer? Yes. Does my card have my e-mail address? No.

People will tell you that they could not exist without their cell phones and their Blackberries, and that they are effective because they have them. If they cannot live without the gadgets, does that mean they couldn't have lived before the machines were born? How did business manage before they were invented? If you want to be successful, you must manage your time and not let it be managed by some gadget.

### The "To Do" List and Your Brain

Almost everyone in business keeps a "To Do" list, but have you ever considered why? If you are engaged in your business and you focus on real issues, you will not forget stuff. So why go through the ritual of writing down your tasks?

Everyone has about the same amount of brain. This is true because our brains are in our heads and all of our heads are approximately the same size. Brains are wired differently from one another. That's why some folks are great pianists, and others scientists, authors, plumbers, or cooks. Therefore it seems logical that our challenge in life is to use what brains we have for the most important things. If you want to call a prospect to offer your product or raise money for your venture, I promise that you will not forget to make that call. When you get up in the morning, you go over all the things you want to do during the day. As you brush your teeth, you go back through the list. While eating breakfast, your brain is going over it once again. Same thing as you drive to work and sit down at your desk. What have you done with the limited brain? Nothing. No great ideas on how to make your company better, or polishing up that new idea, or coming up with a new plan to raise capital. Nothing.

That's why I keep a "To Do" list. So I don't have to take up brain space thinking about them. I write things down and refer to the list only to schedule time to accomplish what I want. I'm never afraid I'm going to forget something important. I start every day with a fresh list carrying things over from the previous day. Often, it is easier to just do something rather than spend the time rewriting the list. Ask my friend, Jerry Gaddis, who ran construction in the apartment days. He says he found it was easier to do stuff than rewrite it. It changed his life.

We type A's are a frustrated lot and find celebration hard to program. Therefore, we must look for small celebrations. Well, here's one. When I have finished doing something on my list, with gusto, I scratch if off. Oh, that feels good. Sometimes I put on my list things that I have already done, just so I can scratch them off.

So, keep a "To Do" list, and keep it for the right reasons. Don't write anything on the list that you are not absolutely committed to doing nor anything that is not important. A "To Do" list of more than half a page is a waste of paper.

# The Signs of a Superstar

I've said a lot about the kind of businesspeople you ought to avoid—the liars, the blamers, the flakes. But there are plenty of superstars out there too—people you want to hire or do business with. How do you identify those people? Superstars show their colors early. You will never have to wonder if they are up to the task. You will never wonder if they are honest. You will know quickly if they have a good work ethic. They will never have to tell you how good they are. People around them will respect them and most will like them. They listen and are thoughtful. Superstars care about people. They are decisive. They get the job done at all levels. They return calls and emails promptly. It's the flakes who are too busy to get back to you.

Here's another way I recognize a superstar: A superstar has really good people working for him or her. Why? First of all, a truly excellent person inspires excellence in others. Second, a superstar isn't afraid that an excellent colleague or employee will take away from his own glory. *her* SHe understands that a rising tide lifts all ships. Take care of your superstars. Compliment them. They'll need some "atta-boys" and pats on the back; it gets lonely at the top. And don't, under any circumstances, micromanage your superstars. That's the surest way to run them off. Let them do their thing, and they will make themselves—and you—rich.

# Lessons from the Boarding Gate

Marilyn and I had a home in Snowmass, Colorado, for more than 35 years. Marilyn and the kids went to the mountains as much as possible—often three months in the summer and two in the winter. My business kept me on the road, but I traveled to the mountains almost every weekend if Marilyn was there. I averaged more than 140 boardings per year on United Airlines alone.

Traveling from Wichita to Aspen was always a challenge. The weather in Aspen was unpredictable; the airlines never seemed sure when flights would leave or arrive—or if they would go at all. Because of the uncertainty of flights, travelers' tempers got very short. Seats were at a premium during weekends in the winter months. I used to stand near the counter just to be entertained by the outrageous conduct. It was a study in human nature—or, in any case, the worst of human nature. I remember one 40-year-old with a pair of ski boots hanging from his neck telling the woman behind the counter, "I am a doctor. I have to get to Aspen immediately to attend to a seriously ill patient." I don't know how many times I heard, "I had a reservation. I don't understand why it's not showing up." Yeah, right.

Almost every week, I saw passengers deriding the person behind the counter, as if it were that person's fault that they couldn't get on the flight they wanted. My favorite incident was on a sunny Sunday winter morning at the Aspen airport. A couple of early flights had been cancelled and the passengers on those flights were milling around the terminal or standing in line trying to change their connecting flights. When early flights are cancelled and all of the other flights are full, things get hairy. A short man about five back from the counter suddenly stepped out of line, looked at the woman behind the counter and, in a very loud voice, exclaimed, "Do you know who I am?" Without missing a beat, the woman behind the counter picked up the mike and said, "May I have your attention please? We have a gentleman in line who doesn't know who he is."

The man's already red face turned purple, and he shouted, "F*** you!"

The gate attendant coolly responded, "You can get in line for that too." The *Denver Post* carried this one. I am glad I watched it happen.

So, what is the lesson here? It reminds me of the song from Mary Poppins, "Just a Spoonful of Sugar Makes the Medicine Go Down." I got to know all of the people at the counters in Wichita, Denver, Aspen, New York, and Chicago. I called them all by name, and they all called me Jack. I treated them with the respect they deserved. And guess what? They never failed to get me on a flight. There is never, ever any reason to raise your voice or blame someone who has no control over a situation, no matter how frustrated you are. It seems too basic a thing to have to mention, but the simple act of treating people behind the counter the way I would expect to be treated made a big impact on them—and on the way they treated me! When you fly, try thanking each of the TSA employees at the security checkpoints as you check in. It makes their day. It might make your day too.

# Hiring and Firing Are Like Sex

In hiring—as in so many other areas of business and life—it's always easier to see the upside when the candidate is on his best behavior, they want and need the job, you need the help, and the positive chemistry is flowing in both directions. The downside tends to be more obvious later. In hiring, remember that the chemistry causes things to get hot and heavy very quickly. Only after the deed is done do you start feeling the regret. That's why I've always said that hiring is like sex. To keep from making mistakes, you must "practice safe hiring." You may have heard the old adage that if you spend 80 percent of your time hiring, you'll only have to spend 20 percent of your time managing. This is true in spades.

Years ago when I was working in my father's real estate office, we had a salesman who could not bring home the bacon. He always needed an advance on the deal that was about to get sold. The real problem with many real estate sales folks is the large amount of money they receive when a deal finally closes. You see, if you live from month to month and believe you will close a deal before you run out of money, you feel that you don't have to work during the month. Well, Danny had that problem big time.

When I hired Danny all was exciting. He needed a job, we needed another sales person. Danny was on his best behavior, wearing his best suit, and I was looking for every good thing I could identify. I was selling him on all of the good things that lay ahead for him. I told him about all the money he was going to make and how selling a couple of houses per month was pretty easy. Danny was adding up all of the money he could make and pouring on the charm. We were selling about two houses a week; a few dollars a month of draws was easy to cover when Danny would sell at least one house a month. WRONG. He had a bad case of salesperson false hope.

Eventually I realized it was time to stop the draw. He was well behind; the time had come to tell him it was over. But I was the one who told him how great it was going to be. I was the one who convinced him to leave his other job. Now I felt that I was the one responsible for his financial world. OUCH. So here is where your brain will not allow you to take the action to fire someone. And by the time you do, it is too late. It comes as no surprise to anyone who works with this person, and if it surprises the person you let go, shame on you. So, what is the lesson here?

First, practice safe hiring. Look for all the reasons you *don't* want to hire the person sitting across the desk. Don't oversell your company to the candidate; you don't want to leave yourself with guilt if it does not work out.

Once you have made the hire, be careful not to elevate the employee to his own level of incompetence. This will set them up for failure easier than anything else you can do. Set clear goals for the employee and go over them frequently, making it clear what you expect. When expectations aren't met, let the person know what you want going forward. If you have to let an employee go, it should never be a surprise to that person.

# Entrepreneur + Manager = Great Team

Value Place, our latest product and franchise system, is run by Greg Kossover. Greg and I have worked together for almost 20 years. Greg is a manager, not an entrepreneur. Together we make one of the best management teams of any company I've been involved in. He's strong at finding great operating people, watching the nickels, and keeping the properties full and squeaky clean. When it comes to major financial decisions, product decisions, new concepts, and even the color of the chairs, that's in my world; Greg couldn't care less. When you put a team together, remember to avoid putting two managers or two entrepreneurs together. Mix them. Two managers will figure, plan and calculate, and nothing will happen. Two entrepreneurs will smile, grin, plan, and promote to their own destruction. Caution, managers without entrepreneurial input will stagnate a mature business. Do not violate this rule.

# Situation Ethics

When you corner a skunk, you could get stink on you. Once, I was involved in a personal investment—not a real estate venture—that taught me a lot about business and human nature. I was dealing with a business that had been around for about 100 years and had gone through bankruptcy a couple of times. The current owners purchased the company out of bankruptcy 11 years before and had produced about ten major projects before I contracted with them. I liked the owner and we became friends while the company worked on my project. We were building a unique project that I was very excited about.

Along the way, signals began to reach my office that vendors were not getting paid in a timely fashion and the company was in a hurry to get the progress draws before they were entitled to them. When my project was about half complete, we still had more than a year to go. I made a big mistake: As I figured that the company was in a rob Peter to pay Paul mode, I was convinced that I was going to be Paul, not Peter, since my project was next to be delivered.

It soon came to light that the company was losing money on my project and delivery had slowed. It was working on other projects so it could get draws to keep the ship afloat.

The company asked me to pay monthly draws instead of progress draws, and I agreed. Wrong again.

Then, unknown to us, they brought in a new investor who got a minority share of the company by putting in needed capital. The financial hole at the

*(continued)*

company was much deeper than any of the customers thought, and so the new investor became the new owner.

Now the players had changed, and the old players switched from telling the truth to telling whatever the new investor wanted to hear. The company's lawyer was also being told what to say and he lost track of the truth.

We received a demand for $5 million to paid immediately for cost overruns—none of which were our issues—or the project, which was now about 80 percent complete, would be stopped. The contracts were very clear; we had done everything and more to live up to our side of the deal.

It was time to get together with everyone at the table. We set up the meeting at their place of business where the lawyers, old guard, and new investor sat at the table. When things get tough in business, true character comes out and the ability to settle anything is gone. We walked out after hearing their outrageous demands and listening to incredible lies from the only member of the old guard who stayed with the company.

Three hundred thousand dollars in attorney bills and four months passed before it was settled. We ended up okay financially, and another lesson was learned. Where there is smoke, you can be sure there is fire. Do not wait when the flags are flying; get to the bottom of the problem right away. Nothing in this kind of scenario ever gets any better if you wait. Truth is gone and without it, life is such that waiting is always wrong. I can think of no instance like this in my business life where it got any better by waiting. Anyone can tell the truth when things are going well, but your true character is defined when you are in a tough situation and still hang on to the truth.

Part III:
Significance

# 9

# Odyssey 88

**M**oving from success to significance is something you must do every day. It is not something you put off for when you have the time or money. Having humility is a very important part of enjoying your move to significance.

The first step in moving from success to significance is simply to stretch your conception of the world you live in. For Marilyn and me, that started with a trip around the world.

Let's begin by a little understanding of where you and I fit in the population of the world. We are told that somewhere near 10 billion people have lived on this Earth and that more than half are still alive. When you look at the blessings bestowed on human beings over the centuries—health, longevity, opportunity, peace, safety, sewer, water, abundant food, respect, freedom, etc.—you and I are the luckiest of the human group. How lucky are we? Well, take a look at these statistics that have been circulated around the Internet for the last couple years. I do not know the precise accuracy of these numbers, but they make a good point.

If we could shrink the Earth's population to 100 people with the ratios that exist today, it would look like this:

60 Asians
12 Europeans
15 from the Western Hemisphere
13 Africans
_____

50 female
50 male
_____

20 white
80 non-white
_____

33 Christian
67 not Christian
_____

20 would earn 89 percent of the world's wealth
25 would live in substandard housing
17 would be unable to read
13 would suffer from malnutrition
_____

2 would have a college education
2 would own a computer

*Fast Company,* April 30, 2001.

Maybe it's time we had another look at our place in the world!

After we sold Residence Inn to Marriott in 1987 and I finished my half-day as a company man, I went home and asked Marilyn what she would like to do. Like most unemployed people, I had plenty of time. I also had one advantage that most unemployed people don't have: a Gulfstream jet.

I don't value leisure, but I do value *earned* leisure. Regular leisure is simply a matter of substituting pleasure for productivity—not a recipe for getting things done. But *earned* leisure is something else entirely. Earned leisure is a reward for productivity. Earned leisure means telling yourself, "When you complete this goal or task, you can enjoy this leisure activity." Earned leisure, therefore, doesn't detract from productivity, but enhances it. And earned leisure is a lot more fun than the kind of leisure that shirks duty and responsibility. It's not accompanied by the nagging sense that you really ought to be doing something else. It's just like when your kids come home with homework and want to watch TV first. If you insist that they do their homework first, they'll enjoy the TV that much more. They won't be looking over their shoulders waiting to see if they're going to get in trouble for wasting time.

After building and selling Residence Inn, Marilyn and I felt that we had earned some serious leisure. We had no idea that our leisure was about to launch us on a whole new life's work. The two of us spent a few weeks discussing our options and decided that what we really wanted to do was see the whole world. Marilyn made a list of all the places in the world she wanted to see; I made a similar list. When we put them side-by-side, we were amazed by how much they were alike. I guess that's what happens when you've been married for 35 years. Both of us wanted to see the world's out-of-the-way places rather than the normal tourist attractions. We wanted to learn about human history over the last 7,000 years—not to mention current events. We had the time and the resources to find out, close up, just what God's world really looks like.

We began planning and hired a travel planner from the West Coast. As the trip began to take shape, we realized that we both wanted to get a feel for the history of mankind. We decided to focus on those places throughout the world where, 7,000 years ago, civilization began taking shape. Many of those places are not especially stable, so we worked with the U.S.

Department of State to understand the security issues. We hired the best guides for several segments of the journey. We had a guide for South America, one for Africa, another for Egypt and the Middle East, one for Asia and one for Russia and the Eastern Bloc. We wanted expert guides, but we didn't necessarily want local guides, who are sometimes biased so that you miss the history and current events of the places you visit.

Our itinerary included 39 countries and all of the continents except Antarctica and Australia. It took more than a year to plan the trip. We collected all the information we could find about our destinations, including any *National Geographic* articles. The Reagan White House cabled all of the embassies in the countries we would visit, sending our arrival dates and asking them to invite us to any activities that might coincide with our time in country. In April 1988 we were finally ready to leave.

The night before our departure, I got a call from the State Department. "Do you have an American flag on the tail of your plane?" the man asked.

"Sure," I said. "Of course I do."

"You might consider painting over it," he said. "You'll be going to some places where the American flag won't be considered a plus ... especially on a private plane."

"I don't know," I said. "It doesn't seem very patriotic."

"We're not going to force you to do anything," the man said. "But I do strongly suggest that you remove the American flag from your plane." I was opposed to the idea, but Marilyn, always the level-headed one, reminded me that we would be putting more than just ourselves in danger if we didn't take the embassy's suggestion.

I thought about what she had said. I thought of everybody who was going to be on our plane over the next four months. It was a tough one, but I called my guys at the hangar and asked them to paint over the flag. Frankly, that was a tough one for me.

Our route was South America to Africa, across the Indian Ocean to Asia and the Pacific, back to the Middle East, up into

Europe, and finally home. The experiences we had during those four months could easily fill a book. It truly was a life-changing experience. From the time I called for the copilot to raise the landing gear in Wichita until we put the gear back down three and a half months later on the approach to West Germany, Marilyn and I were always in the minority—something we were not accustomed to. We were in the minority because we are white, Christian, and free. All too often, we take that for granted.

It was sobering to learn that the things we take for granted put us in the minority in the vast majority of the world. We knew it, of course, but we hadn't truly experienced it until we had gone to dozens of out-of-the-way, totally non-touristy corners of the world. We found that the most important need in the world isn't food or money or even freedom, but hope. Anyone who makes such a journey will be overwhelmed by the lack of hope in so many parts of the world. And yet, we were amazed at the kindness, generosity, and resourcefulness of people even in places that seemed hopeless.

The first leg of our journey took us to Mexico and then to the Amazon Basin. For hours, we soared over the Amazon's green-carpeted expanses veined with small rivers leading to the big artery of the Amazon River. We finally landed in Manaus, a city not accessible by road but that was populated by more than one million people!

Traveling on the Amazon was an interesting prologue to the trip, being that our theme was the beginnings of civilization. There are many places on that river that look exactly as they did long before civilization. It was like starting with a blank slate: After getting a look at a world without civilization, we were about to launch into our tour of civilization's beginnings. Of course, we also saw places on the Amazon where "civilization" was a little too evident—places where the rain forest had been cut down or burned with no real planning or reforestation efforts. The Basin looks lush, but the soil is actually not very fertile. The locals cut down areas of trees to burn them in order to put nutrients back into the soil. But after a couple of years, the nutrients are gone, so they stop growing there and move on to a new area.

We had three great days on the river. We did it all, from hacking our way through the jungle to trapping caiman. At night, it was the darkest place I had ever seen—or perhaps I should say the darkest place I had *never* seen. We seemed to be a world away from the nearest electric light. We boated to the spot where the jet-black water of the Rio Negro mingles with the orange water of the Solimões to form the real beginning of the Amazon.

From the river, we flew to the coast of Brazil, then crossed the Atlantic to the Ivory Coast and Kenya where we went on a safari. The U.S. Embassy in the Ivory Coast suggested that flying across Zaire, though the shortest route to Kenya, could be problematic. So after refueling in Gabon, we shut off the radios and crossed Zaire at 43,000 feet, and landed in Nairobi, Kenya. After a stop at Victoria Falls on the Zambezi River on the border of Zambia and Zimbabwe, we went to South Africa, where I gave a lecture at the University of Cape Town. It was the first time I told my story of ego, collapse, and recovery on the continent of Africa!

Those were the days of the international embargo against South Africa. We each carried two U.S. passports because a South Africa stamp could get us barred from several other countries. In addition, any aircraft taking off from South Africa had a hard time getting official clearance to land in certain other African nations, including Tanzania—the next stop on our itinerary.

As I mentioned earlier, I believe in asking for forgiveness rather than permission. I wasn't in any mood to make multiple stops to complete our flight to Tanzania. So we flew across southern Africa at 41,000 feet and shut off the radio for some time. Then we filed for clearance so that our friends in Tanzania wouldn't know we were coming from South Africa.

Dar Es Salaam was one of the grimmest places we visited on our world tour. We never left the airport. It's amazing to think that Tanzania contains perhaps the oldest continuously inhabited areas on Earth. Marilyn and I were both glad to lift off and head to the beautiful Seychelles in the Indian Ocean. From the urban ugliness of Dar Es Salaam to the lush beauty of the Seychelles, we were once again struck by the huge disparities in the way people live throughout the world.

We hopped across the Indian Ocean to Indonesia, landing in Ujung Padang and riding nine hours in a van—mostly at night on narrow roads through scary places—to Torajaland, famous for its burial caves and unique embalming customs that result in corpses staying preserved for decades. From there we went to Brunei, where the Sultan, thanks to liquefied gas sales to Japan, has become one of the richest men in the world. The locals told us that the next day would be a holiday if the Sultan saw the moon that night. It was cloudy, so the next day was a normal workday. The Sultan's main house was built by the U.S. construction company Bechtel and cost one billion dollars. It overlooks the water and people who, for hundreds of years, have lived on the river in a terrible slum. In Jakarta, Marilyn and I decided to play some tennis. We ended up playing Indonesia's national mixed doubles champions—an embarrassing but otherwise enjoyable experience.

From Indonesia we flew to the Pacific Islands that were made famous during World War II—Guadalcanal, New Britain, and Bouganville. I had one particular goal in mind: I wanted to see the Mitsubishi GM4—a.k.a. Betty Bomber—that Admiral Yamamoto was killed in. In one of the most dramatic missions of the war in the Pacific, a squadron of American P-38s had been sent from Guadalcanal to intercept and shoot down the airplane that, according to American code-breakers, carried the ever-punctual Yamamoto. Eighteen fighters screamed a couple of hundred miles across the Pacific, outmaneuvered the six Zeroes that were escorting the Admiral's plane, and shot it out of the sky. The plane crashed in the jungle on the island of Bouganville.

We had heard that Yamamoto's Betty Bomber was still there in the jungle; we chartered two helicopters to take us to see it. We flew to the area and met the local king, who gave us permission to fly one of the helicopters into the area where the plane had gone down more than 40 years earlier. We located the wreckage and descended into the jungle through trees that stood higher than a hundred feet tall. The rotors of the helicopter were cutting branches as we settled onto the jungle floor. From what I understand, the video we took on that trip was later a part of the display at the Boeing Air Museum in Seattle. It was an incredible experience to stand there in the sticky heat of a Pacific jungle and take in the scene where such dramatic events had taken place.

But that wasn't the most dramatic moment during our time in the Pacific Islands—not even close. On the island of New Britain in Papua New Guinea, we witnessed a fire dance. This wasn't a show they put on for tourists. This was the real thing: Men and women dancing through a fire so huge that I thought it was going to singe my eyebrows from several yards away.

Before the dance, four men from our party followed the native men into the jungle to watch them prepare to walk through a white-hot fire. It was a cloudy night, and the only light came from a Coleman lantern—ironic, I thought, since Coleman is a Wichita company. The men covered their bodies with a black, gloppy paint that looked like tar. They also cut themselves and used their blood to draw figures on large panels that they would take to the fire dance. They were chewing betel nut, a mild stimulant, but not a hard drug—certainly not the kind of thing that would cause a person not to feel the heat of a fire.

When their preparations were complete, the men put out the lamp and disappeared, leaving us four white guys alone in the jungle in pitch darkness as a light rain began to fall. It was one of the more stressful moments of our tour. We followed the sound of the native drums toward the clearing where the fire was roaring. Marilyn and Cousin Betty were waiting there.

As the drums pounded, the men waved the blood-decorated panel and held a huge boa constrictor. They danced around the fire that reached much higher than their heads, and then danced through the white-hot coals! We wouldn't have believed it if we hadn't seen it with our own eyes. This was not a small fire, and the men didn't dash quickly through it. They took their time dancing. As I said, this wasn't a show they were putting on for us, though they were gracious enough to let us watch. This was their culture's way of proving their manhood. We were told that the most heroic dancer would have his choice of the tribal women. Amazing what a guy might do to meet a woman.

And, as it turned out, not only manhood was being tested but womanhood too. We watched a woman carrying a small child dance around the fire then walk through it—with the child in her arms. Our guide told us that she was trying to exorcise the demons from her sick child. I have never seen anything like it before or since.

I've thought about that native woman and what her fire dance meant. Say what you want about the wisdom of walking a small child through a huge fire, but she is a woman who, in her way, was putting first things first. She knew what was important to her, and she made her choices accordingly. She put aside every other concern and fear and did what she believed to be necessary. I've heard people say, "I'd walk through fire for my children," but I have actually seen somebody who did it. I hope it helped the child.

From the Pacific Islands, our next stop was China. The Chinese wouldn't let us fly into China as private aviators, so we left the Gulfstream in Hong Kong and flew to Beijing on Cathay Pacific Airlines. Our guide for the Asian leg of our journey was Barry Till, the curator for the Asian Art Museum in Victoria, British Columbia. Barry was a joy to travel with. He was a graduate of the university in Beijing. His Mandarin

Chinese was perfect, which opened up exactly the kinds of experiences we were looking for on our non-touristy tour of the world. We could stop anywhere on the road, go up to a Chinese home, knock on the door, and ask if we could come in and chat. We met some very interesting people to say the least. And I think they found us interesting too.

Driving on a country road, we stopped at a small single-family house and knocked on the door. An elderly woman came to the door and after a conversation with Barry, she invited us in. We sat in her small living area where a framed photo of her son in uniform was displayed. She explained that he was a soldier in Korea during the war in the 1950's. I had been a U.S. soldier at that same time—a fact that we did not mention to this frail woman who was being so gracious to us. It's strange that humans can be arch enemies dedicated to killing each other at one time, and then just 36 years later, be chatting comfortably as new-found friends. I guess we will never learn.

We hired a Russian helicopter to fly us over the Great Wall. It had 20 seats, and there were only six of us, so we thought we would have lots of room. Wrong. The Chinese decided to add some folks to our flight, and that presented a problem. I had been taking video of our whole trip, and I definitely wanted video of the Great Wall. The problem was that the Chinese government didn't allow people to take aerial photos of the Great Wall. Barry somehow convinced all the Chinese people to go to the front of the helicopter and kept them occupied while I recorded video of the Wall.

From there we went to Xian to see the famous Terra Cotta army around the tomb of the first Ming emperor. This was another place where video cameras weren't allowed, but Barry and I figured out how I could tape inconspicuously from my hip with him standing close. There was a little standalone building near the excavation site with a scale model of a beautiful carriage with a team of horses. It was gorgeous with copper and

Cloisonné and beautifully lighted in a darkened room. I could not resist taking video of that too.

Instantly, four soldiers grabbed me and took me to a small room where they insisted that I surrender the camera to them. I was very glad to see that Barry followed us to the interrogation room. I told Barry to get the film, and not to worry about the camera. He explained to the soldiers that I didn't have any footage that violated their rules. Unfortunately, one of the soldiers was a camera whiz and turned ours on to show us that we had indeed broken all sorts of rules.

Then the negotiation started in earnest. I pulled two $100 bills out of my wallet. I didn't offer them to anybody, mind you. That would be bribery. I was just looking at it. The soldier had the camera in his hand. I had $200 in my hand. He grabbed the money. I grabbed the camera. He grabbed the camera back. I grabbed the money back (this was very sophisticated negotiation we were doing). Somehow the soldier ended up with both the money and the camera.

Now it was Barry's turn to negotiate. Once again, I told him to get the film if possible. Incredible as it seems, he got them to agree to return the camera and the film as long as we promised to erase the images when we got back to the hotel. *Sure*, I thought. *As long as you promise to give that money to charity.* But I didn't say it out loud. Those images make up an interesting part of the 40 hours of video I have from the trip. It was amazing what American cash could accomplish in China in those days.

There was a lot to love about China, but there was also a lot about China that made me love the United States more than I already did. There was a strange combination of stifling bureaucracy and make-it-up-as-you-go-along freewheeling that's hard to imagine until you see it in action.

Take, for instance, our experience with the Mao Jeeps. In Beijing, we visited a plant where they made the Jeeps that you used to see Mao Tse Tung riding in, waving to the crowd. I thought it would be fun to have one. So after eating lunch with some of the company officers, I asked the head of the plant if I could purchase one of the Jeeps. He said yes, it would be possible. My son, Sky, suggested we buy two so we could have one for parts. At a mere $2,000 apiece, that wasn't a bad idea. The challenge, as it turned out, wasn't so much buying the Jeeps as getting them out of China and into Kansas. It took about three years to get them. But what could we do? And at $2,000, who can complain?

But I digress. Ironically, buying two Jeeps in China was nothing compared to trying to license them. Sure, having two Chinese Jeeps would be fun, but wouldn't it be more fun to have Chinese plates for them?

Barry and I set out to buy plates. Our first stop was a neighborhood police station. They were very polite, but they explained that we couldn't buy the plates without the Jeeps. "But we're waiting on the Jeeps to be delivered," Barry explained in his impeccable Chinese. The officer smiled and nodded but didn't budge. He did, however, tell us about another police station where they might be able to help. The people at the second station were just as polite as those at the first—and just as unhelpful. They sent us to a third police station. More smiling. More nodding. And then they suggested that we go to another station—the first one we had tried! The old Chinese Triangle was working overtime that day.

Not to be outdone, Barry and I talked to a taxi driver about getting the plates. We should have started there instead of getting sucked into the bureaucratic vortex. The taxi driver was a can-do type of guy. He said he would meet us at 7:00 the next morning with two license plates that would cost us $75 USD each. There he was outside our hotel at 7:00 the next morning, with two license plates. One had come off a general's car, he said, so it would cost a little extra. *Yeah, right*, I thought. But I paid it. I wanted the plates more than I wanted a few extra dollars.

We had flown commercial into China, so we had to go through airport security to get out of there. In the security line, I remembered the big, heavy, metal license plates in my bag. I thought there was a good chance that they would attract the attention of the security scanners. But security, if you'll excuse the pun, was like a Chinese fire drill that day. I pushed the bag with the plates around the arch of the metal detector and picked it up on the other side. Nobody seemed to notice—or, in any case, to care—and we got out of the country in good shape.

After a visit to southeast Asia (which will be the subject of the next chapter), we went on to the Middle East. We flew over the Straits of Hormuz and into Yemen on July 2, 1988. Sixteen hours later, on the morning of July 3, the U.S. Navy mistakenly shot down an Iranian Airbus over the strait, killing 290 people. It was a terrible tragedy, and it made for a few tense days for Americans in the Middle East.

Thanks to an introduction from the Reagan White House, we were invited to the U.S. Ambassador's residence for a Fourth of July party. Besides diplomats from countries all over the world, Soviet army and Air Force officers attended the party. Strange as it seems, even though the Cold War was ongoing, the Soviets and Americans shared an airfield in Yemen. Imagine what a strange party that was: Armed guards on every rooftop, uncertainty about what was going to happen next in a region that has never been very stable, and we're rubbing shoulders with Russian military a day after our military has shot down a civilian aircraft of one of their allies.

Meanwhile, I was thinking about what might happen when we flew out the next morning. I didn't know what the risks might be. I spoke with the U.S. Marine Captain who was in charge of the protection detail. His advice was to dash over into Saudi airspace as soon as possible after takeoff. "Nobody around here screws with the Saudis," he said. "But I don't think anybody's going to mess with you anyway," he said. "You're nobody."

I've never been so glad to be nobody.

From the Middle East we went to Europe for the last leg of the trip. I already mentioned how depressing Dar Es Salaam was. I'd put Cold War Moscow at a close second. One day I left our security folks and walked alone in the residential areas and through the halls of residential apartment buildings. No one ever looked me in the eye or spoke. The buildings looked like they were going to fall down and smelled like sour cabbage. In the busy streets, it seemed the only people who spoke or even looked at me were looking to exchange money illegally or sell sex. That kind of black-market activity was worse in Moscow than anywhere else in the world we had been. I'm convinced that democracy didn't work in post-Soviet Russia simply because democracy can't work without basic morality. Few things have ever made me happier to be an American than our visit to Moscow before the Wall came down.

After several stops in Western Europe (including a visit with our friends in Germany), we flew back across the Atlantic. We were home again, among familiar people and places. We weren't in the minority any more. And yet, so much had changed.

Our four-month experience could fill a whole book. But this isn't about the trip of a lifetime but a trip *through* a lifetime and the lessons along the way. The most life-impacting day of that trip is the subject of the next chapter.

# What Happened to My 727?

After our trip around the world, our trip planner convinced me to buy a Boeing 727 and configure it all first-class for high-end travel to exotic places in the world. The idea was to have a business booking tours for wealthy clients. It was another case of seeing only the upside of a business proposition and finding out the downside after it was too late. After taking a five million dollar write off, I sold the jet to TAESA airline in Mexico. I carried the note. At first, payments came in regularly. But then they stopped. I flew to Mexico City to get the money and came home with some of the money, but I started to get a little nervous.

I had a loan on the airplane at Chase Bank in New York. One day, my loan officer called and asked me if I had seen the *Wall Street Journal* that morning. I hadn't so he read me an article from the front page about drugs being flown in from South America to remote fields in Mexico before being flown on to the United States in a smaller aircraft. The article specifically mentioned TAESA 727s. "I'm concerned," the loan officer said. I asked him to hold. I called my insurance agent to ask if I was insured if a foreign government confiscated the airplane. He said I was. I went back to the loan officer and said, "No problem." It never came to that, but the whole episode made me realize that I was out of my league.

Later, a couple of my guys went to Mexico and found the airplane in heavy maintenance. No engines were to be found. Fortunately I had a good lawyer

*(continued)*

when we made the deal, and I was finally able to get the balance of the money owed to me.

The lesson? I'm not sure there is one. But the story is too good not to tell.

# Celebrate Leisure

My dad always said there is never a convenient time to take a vacation. Like me, my dad was a Type-A who found it difficult to enjoy leisure time. Dad never put on old clothes except once or twice a year when he went fishing. Dad always was dressed to work: white shirt, tie, etc. I always admired his work ethic, but now I understand what his drive cost him. I now consider *earned* leisure to be a key part of my working life. When I have a goal to accomplish in business, I set a timetable. And that timetable includes a celebration of success. For years, I felt that I did not have the time to celebrate so I didn't do it. I guess that goes back to wanting the world to know that any success I had came as result of my hard work. Nuts. I think about Jimmy Carter who always carried a brief case full of papers and was working on details of all kinds. Jimmy Carter is the ultimate Type-A. Even now that he's retired, he still seems to always be busy. Then I think of Ronald Reagan, who never carried anything, but was always able to focus on a few important things. You tell me who was the more effective president.

# 10

# Burma

The course of a life can change in a matter of hours. For Marilyn and me, an eventful 24 hours in Burma utterly transformed the way we think about the world and our place in it. We both believe that it was God at work to place us in Burma at precisely the right time and change both of our lives forever. We had experienced the joys of moving from success to significance in many small ways for the past 20 years, but this was Earth shaking.

In the previous chapter, I skipped over our experiences in Burma because I wanted to give Burma (which changed its name to Myanmar in 1989) its own chapter. Yes, those four months abroad changed us, but it was our 24 hours in Burma that really changed us.

Burma had been a closed country for decades, run by the same military dictatorship since the early '60s. As far as the Western world was concerned, Burma was a mystery, and the Burmese government liked it that way. They kept the country in a rapidly deteriorating isolation, refusing all offers of help from the West.

Tucked between China, India, and Thailand, Burma was Asia's rice bowl at the beginning of World War II. Thanks to British investments in their infrastructure, they appeared to be making progress toward joining the world community after the War. But the high-profile assassination of Aung San (father of the pro-democracy activist Aung San Suu Kyi) marked the end of Burma's embrace of the wider world. By the 1980s, half of the deaths in that country of 45 million were children under the age of five. They were dying of dysentery and malaria, diseases that can be cured with a trip to the corner Walgreens in this country.

The ever-resourceful Barry Till somehow convinced Burma's dictatorship to allow us into the country. We landed in the capital city of Rangoon (which, like the country's name, would change in 1989 ... to Yangon). As was my custom, I pulled out my video camera and started taping as soon as we got off the plane. As was the Burmese custom, a soldier informed me that video cameras were not allowed in the country. One quick look at his AK-47 convinced me that this wasn't something I wanted to fight over. I quickly apologized and said I would stash the camera on the plane immediately.

But, of course, I couldn't possibly go into a place like Burma and not get any film footage. I knew the security people were much more lenient with crew searches than with passenger searches, so I gave the camera to one of the crew members and asked him to bring it to the hotel for me.

Having landed around noon, we were driven to our assigned hotel to eat lunch and meet the security people and guides who had been assigned to us. The hotel was a tired old Russian-built structure on beautiful Inya Lake. At lunch, our waiter carried a fly swatter under his arm and very kindly killed the flies on our plates while we ate.

The plan was to tour the city of Rangoon after lunch. But our handlers told us that the tour had to be cancelled on account of a student uprising downtown. *A student uprising?* I thought. *I've never seen a student uprising!* It wouldn't be safe, our guide said. There were hundreds of students in the streets, facing off against police and military units determined to keep the peace.

"But we've come all the way to Burma from the other side of the world," I said. "Do we really have to stay in the hotel all day?"

"I'm afraid so," the guide said in her broken English. "It's for your safety."

"But what about the Schwedegon Pagoda?" I said. "Can we at least see the Schwedagon Pagoda?"

The guide thought on it for a minute. The Burmese are extremely proud of the Schwedagon Pagoda, and rightly so. It's the most elaborate and ornate house of worship in the world, and the most sacred Buddhist temple in Burma. Its tallest spire stands almost 400 feet high, and the whole structure is covered in gold. For at least 1,000 years—and likely for 1,500—the Schwedagon Pagoda has dominated Rangoon's horizon.

"Well ..." the guide said. "The Schwedagon is a few miles from the area where the students are protesting." It was obvious that she wanted to show us Rangoon's greatest wonder. "I suppose we could go to the Schwedagon and come right back."

We hired two taxis—1962 Chevy Impalas—to take the four of us and the guide to the Pagoda. Except for official vehicles, 1962 models were the newest cars on the road. Driving through the streets of Rangoon was like going back in time, or being in a movie set in 1962. What few cars we passed were from the '50s or early '60s.

The Pagoda was breathtaking, but I couldn't stop thinking about that student protest. The Pagoda had an incredible history, but on the other side of town, I thought, history might be in the making. I asked the taxi driver to drive through downtown on the way back to the hotel. He shot a nervous look at our guide. She didn't say anything, but she gave a barely perceptible nod. I've since wondered why she allowed us to go where we could see the protests. As a representative of the Burmese government, it was her job to *prevent* us from seeing things like that. I suspect she did it because she loved Burma more than she loved the Burmese government. I believe that, whatever her official responsibilities, she *wanted* somebody from the outside world to see what was happening to her country.

Rangoon's narrow streets grew more crowded the closer we got to downtown. The streets were alive with soldiers carrying weapons. There were tanks and trucks on every corner. Marilyn was more than a little nervous, and I wasn't feeling all that relaxed myself. Here was the police state in action. Our driver scanned left and right, left and right, alert to the growing tension around us. I could tell he was assessing and re-assessing escape routes if things got uglier.

The air was heavy with expectation. Something big was looming, like a thunderhead about to burst. I pulled out my video camera and, as stealthily as I could, captured a few minutes of film, recording the frightening scene before us. Our guide pretended she didn't see the camera.

Waves of students were chanting and marching, waving signs and yelling at the soldiers, who fingered their semi-automatics. Ironically, it seemed there was more fear in the eyes of the soldiers than in the eyes of the unarmed protesters. Most of the soldiers had no desire to shoot down their own countrymen for the sake of a repressive regime.

We didn't witness any violence that day, but the riots of 1988 were on. Those May protests were early rumblings of the movement that came to be known as the 8888 Popular Uprising. On August 8, 1988 (8/8/88, hence the name), students and Buddhist monks led widespread protests that resulted in a government crackdown and thousands of deaths. It was the 8888

Uprising, in fact, that brought the well-known activist Aung San Suu Kyi to prominence.

We safely made it back to our hotel that evening. At seven p.m. all hotel guests were locked inside. Thank goodness there wasn't a fire that night! That night, we were told, 11 people were killed near our hotel.

The next morning, a car picked us up to take us to our chartered wreck of a boat to tour the Ayeyarwady River—as if nothing had happened. Our guide was joined by two more young men who spoke excellent English. At first we didn't know what it meant; had our handlers decided we needed extra "supervision?" But as it turned out, those two young men were one of the best things that happened during our short stay in Burma. As we talked with them throughout the day, they helped us make sense of what we were seeing in the country and make a real connection with the land and its people.

We motored upriver two hours, arriving at the village of Twante, where many of Burma's clay pots are made. We loaded into three pony carts pulled by the most emaciated horses I've ever seen. Their poke-ribbed misery was a metaphor for everything we saw around us. The locals lined the dirty streets to stare at us. No doubt we were the first white people many of them had ever seen.

After several hours in Twante, we boarded the boat for our return to Rangoon. It was then that our two new handlers began to open up to us. "Burma is a ruin. We have no hope," they said. They told story after story of suffering and hardship—hunger, repression, hopelessness. Their lives were miserable and there were plenty of people in Burma who had it worse than they did. We had seen plenty of squalor on our travels, but this was the first time we spoke with people who lived in genuine poverty and repression. It was the first time we really experienced the human face of that kind of suffering. "Our parents are always apologizing to us," they said. "They say they're sorry for what happened in 1960. When our parents were our age, Burma had a real chance to join the free world. Now Burma is a place of decadence and decay. There is no hope here. No way out."

Marilyn and I can point to that two-hour boat ride as a true turning point in our lives. Witnessing such misery and hopelessness up close, we realized that we couldn't just look at it and not get involved. We were no longer observers of Burma's sorrow; we became participants in it. We had been blessed with so much, so much, in fact, that we could easily insulate ourselves from the troubles that plague so much of the world's population. But those two hours on the boat with two young Burmese men made us realize that we couldn't isolate or insulate. We had made a human connection. Burma's troubles weren't statistics. They were people—people not so different from us. We weren't yet sure what we were going to do, but we knew we had to do something. The conditions in Burma were some of the worst in the world, but there were three billion people living in countries where the conditions weren't a whole lot better.

When we got back to our hotel, the young people at the front desk rushed up to us with a message from the U.S. Embassy: "You must leave the country immediately. We can no longer guarantee your safety. Your flight crew has already left for the airport." We rushed around and packed as quickly as we could, but I did take the time to break down my video camera into several pieces, the better to hide it from the prying eyes of government security personnel.

The drive back to the airport was like nothing we had ever seen. A monsoon-like rain pelted down on the few cars headed out of town. The official cars were speeding out of the city, but the rest of the cars barely moved. We passed trucks filled with soldiers and old 1960 buses with people hanging off the back and out of every window.

When we finally got to the airport, it felt exactly like a black and white Humphrey Bogart movie. It was dark, dank, and teeming with people trying to leave the country. We pushed our way through the crowd to Security and Immigration. When we were one camera short of the count they took when we entered the country, the tension began to mount. Realizing that I had intentionally over counted when we arrived to cover for the video camera, I flashed a tape recorder that Marilyn and I had used throughout the trip to recount our experiences. They passed us on toward the door to the airline ramp. Then, two young soldiers stopped us and pointed machine guns at us. Our guide Barry Till was prepared. First he tried to push them aside saying, "Private flight, private flight," but they did not budge. It was time for some good old-fashioned bribery. With a little exchange, we passed through to the outside. Our exchange was whisky, cigarettes, and playing cards with adult pictures. Barry knew what we would need if things did not go well. As the Boy Scouts say, "Be prepared."

Only two airplanes were on the tarmac, a Russian airliner and our Gulfstream. The rain continued as we awoke the driver of a 40-year-old bus to take us out to the airplane. The crew was waiting. They opened the door as we scrambled up the stairs and into our seats. The moment we closed the door, a military vehicle with flashing lights on top pulled up in front of the plane and a soldier got out. He stood in the pouring rain and signaled for us to open the door.

The soldier was young—not much more than a boy, really. His much too-big uniform swallowed him, making him look younger than he probably was. But even a boy is somebody to listen to when he's pointing a gun in your direction. He stood in the driving rain and signaled for us to open the door and put down the stairs. I didn't like the thought of opening the door to a man with a gun, but we didn't have any choice. The soldier came up the stairs to the inside. He eyed each of the people in the plane and fingered his gun. We nervously looked at the soldier, at each other, and then back to the soldier. Finally, in pretty good English, he spoke. "You got Chocolate?"

I didn't know if we had chocolate or not. Tense moments followed as I went to the galley in the rear. Thankfully, I turned up a package of Oreo cookies. When we had new people join us along the way, we always asked them to bring cash, Oreos, popcorn, and Progresso soup. I handed the cookies to him, not sure if it was going to be adequate. The soldier smiled and went back down the stairs. We closed the door once again and started the engines, saved by a package of Oreo cookies.

As we taxied out to the only runway, we were told that there was an inbound Russian aircraft and we would have to wait for takeoff until its arrival. Military vehicles were moving about the airport, the rain still hammering the aircraft as we waited. The wind was calm, so we were not sure which direction the inbound aircraft was arriving from. Standing on the taxiway at the departure end of the runway, the pilots and I agreed that if we saw a military vehicle coming toward us, we were going to take off, permission or not. The ceiling was about 100 feet, and the visibility was less than a quarter of a mile, so we would disappear in a very short time after takeoff. About that time, to our amazement, we received our takeoff clearance. Climbing into the clouds as the gear came up was a time for jubilant celebration.

Before our trip, I was feeling good about my chances of the day when I would meet my Maker. "Well, Jack," I pictured him saying, "how did you do?" I felt confident in my ability to say, "Well, Lord, I did a pretty good job—not perfect, of course, but acceptable, I hope. I did most of the things my parents asked me. I was an adequate student. I went to college as my mother expected. I went into the Army during the Korean War. I came out of the service, worked with my father for a few years and started several companies. I wasn't always successful in those companies, but I didn't cheat people, and I took good care of my employees. I was the breadwinner for my family and they never went without. I attended church, sang the songs, and said the prayers. Not too bad I guess."

But on our return from this incredible journey, it occurred to me that God will ask a different question, and He might not be so happy with my answer. "Jack," he will say, "I gave you good health, a fine family, an education, resources, and the ability to communicate. I made you free and called you to become a Christian. I gave you longevity and good friends. I kept you safe from harm and provided a very happy life ... Right?"

"Yes."

"So what did you do for my planet and its inhabitants who were in real need?"

Whoops.

---

What *was* I going to do for those who were in real need? I had spent 40 years living for myself. I had spent the next 20 years living for my business. But living for other people? I was going to need some help on that one. When we returned to Wichita, we invited nine couples from various walks of life to come to a seven-course dinner at a nice restaurant. The group included a banker, a Boeing worker, a minister, a couple of friends, an insurance agent, the then president of Pizza Hut, and others. Some of them we knew well, some we were acquainted with, and a few we didn't know at all. While they ate, Marilyn and I talked about our trip—what we had seen and what it had meant to us. We told them many of the stories you read in the last chapter. We showed some of the video—not all 40 hours, fortunately for them.

When we were finished with our travelogue, I told our guests that they were going to have to pay for their dinner. We got a couple of nervous looks; it was a pretty nice dinner! But then I explained that the price of the dinner was going to be a letter. We asked that each couple, in light of what we had just told them, write and tell us how they thought we ought to make a difference in the wider world. We knew we weren't smart enough to figure it out on our own. But those nine other couples would have 18 different perspectives on what's really important about giving back.

Nine couples from nine different walks of life. We were a little afraid of what we might get back. There's such a thing as too much good advice. But the amazing thing about those nine letters was how similar they were. It was as if we were getting a sign from God himself. Of course there were different emphases, but everyone told us the following:

- Find a passion.
- Don't start something new.
- Support and get involved with an existing organization you believe in.

The passion was already taking shape. We knew that Burma had captured our hearts. And we could easily see the wisdom in not starting something new. But how were we going to identify the organization that we could plug into?

A few days later, we received a call from Frank Kik, the minister of Eastminster Presbyterian Church, who had come to our dinner. He said that Bob Seiple, the President of World Vision, would be in town and would like to have lunch with Marilyn and me.

We met Bob at the Wichita Country Club for lunch. Bob told us about World Vision, and a whole new chapter opened up for Marilyn and me. It was as if our new passion was finding the place where it could find feet and hands.

Bob is now a member of the DeBoer Family Foundation board and a really good friend. I have always accused Bob and Frank of setting us up. The President of World Vision just happened to be in Wichita a week or two after Frank had been at our dinner? Sure, I believe that. Sometimes even men of the cloth tell a stretcher or two. That lunch marked the beginning of our involvement with World Vision.

# Our Man in Burma

On one trip to Burma, we were invited to meet Aung San Suu Kyi at the Charge residence with Congressman Tony Snow, who was in country at the time. We went to the Ambassadors residence at the appointed time, excited to meet Aung San Suu Kyi, only to find out that she was early and had just left. We didn't get to meet her. The congressman was expounding on how difficult and intractable she was. Suu Kyi didn't really like what we were doing in Burma to help the people because our money was going, partly, to the government. It was her belief that the Burmese people should be left alone until they can't stand the oppression any more and rise up in revolt.

Congressman Snow told us that Senator Mitch McConnell was Suu Kyi's contact in DC, and that because of her influence, McConnell was in favor of stopping any U.S. involvement. When we returned, I called Senator Bob Dole, a friend, and he arranged for us to see Senator McConnell. Marilyn and I went to his office. He entered the office—as I am sure all legislators do from time to time—with a "how long is this going to take" look on his face. We told him we were not going to ask the government for anything, but that we had put several million dollars into Burma to help children, and we understood that one of his staff was communicating with Suu Kyi and that he was considering putting an end to any U.S. efforts. We explained much of what World Vision was doing in Burma and what our goals and accomplishments were. The Senator sat down, relaxed, and listened. Then he asked how he

*(continued)*

could help. I suggested he go to Burma with us and see for himself. To our surprise, he said he would.

We left on a high note and then began to arrange for a visa for Senator McConnell. Nope. The Burmese government didn't want any part of that. Try as we might, we were not able to get a visa for the senator. A few months later, World Vision received a check from the U.S. Government for $250,000 to support its efforts in Burma. We do not know why or how, but the check cleared.

# The Pigeon Blood Ruby

When my Saudi friend, Yousef, learned that I was returning to Burma, he called and asked me to look for a Pigeon Blood Ruby of around ten carats. I had no idea what a Pigeon Blood Ruby was, but I told him I would see what I could do. Burma is the source of many of the world's finest jewels, including, I found out later, the Pigeon Blood Ruby. On our way to Burma, Marilyn and I stopped in Bangkok and visited a fancy jewelry store to learn what we could about this ruby. The manager told us that a ten-carat would be difficult, if not impossible, to get; if I could find one, he said, it would be priced in the neighborhood of $100,000 per carat. I was shocked and a little concerned about my search.

When we arrived in Burma, I explained to our Burmese friends what I wanted. They took me to the market, where we went from shop to shop and finally up a back stair to a small room where an elderly Chinese man sat at a small desk. He asked me how I planned to pay for the gem. I explained that I would bring a gemologist, and once we knew the quality, we would pay in any way he wanted the money. He told me he had a gem of about ten carats that was not absolutely perfect, but it could be cut to a perfect nine carats. I told him I would talk to my friend and get back to him.

That night we had dinner with our friend, the Burmese General. I asked him about my search for the gem. He told me that he would introduce me to the Minister of Mines. The next day, Marilyn and I trav-

*(continued)*

eled to the offices of the Minister of Mines, where we were met by four or five young Burmes. They took us up four flights of stairs to a large room where the walls were lined with jewels in cases. In the center of the room was a table for tea and cookies and cashew nuts. There we waited for the Minister.

When the door at the end of the room opened, Marilyn and I gasped. The Minister of Mines was our Chinese friend. He did not acknowledge us and we did not acknowledge him. He showed us a one-carat Pigeon Blood Ruby; compared to regular rubies, it was like fire when he put the light on it. He invited us to come in February to the Emporium where Burma sells jewels to world vendors to raise hard currency.

When I returned to Bangkok, I called my friend in Saudi Arabia and told him he had sent a boy to do a man's work. I offered to return with his gem expert if he wished me to do that. I saw him in Geneva about six months later, and he told me he had purchased an eight-carat Pigeon Blood Ruby for his wife.

# World Vision

T he advice we got on our return from Odyssey 88 was simple: Find a passion, don't start anything new, and plug into an existing organization that we believed in. That organization turned out to be World Vision. The more we have dealt with them, the more firmly we believe in the work they're doing. Thanks to World Vision, our resources and energies have been able to make a big difference in Burma. We had seen a large part of the world and knew of the incredible needs everywhere. World Vision looks at the world and says, "We will make a difference, one child at a time." This was something Marilyn and I could understand and get involved in.

After the dinner in Wichita, Bob Seiple, the president of World Vision, invited Marilyn and me to join a group that was going to Guatemala to see a World Vision operation in the field. The group included Fred Fetterolf, the president of Alcoa, and his wife Fran, who are still close friends of ours. The Fetterolfs

189

were very involved in World Vision; they helped us understand more about what was to become the largest humanitarian organization in the world. We flew down to Guatemala City with Frank Kik, the pastor of Eastminster Presbyterian Church, along with his wife Phyllis, both of whom had attended the nine-couple dinner a short time before.

In Guatemala City, we visited a dump where a whole subsociety lives, sorting through the trash from the city, trying to make a life out of other people's leavings. World Vision had a safe house on the edge of the dump. There we saw World Vision team members put their arms around children from the dump—children who had nobody else in the world to hold or take care of them. We went into the countryside to visit a village where World Vision employees and volunteers were operating an ADP (Area Development Program). At this particular ADP, World Vision had installed a clean water system, a corn processing facility, a health clinic, and a school.

The operation was impressive. I know how hard it is to keep a complex organization running; it is truly an accomplishment to keep things running smoothly in another country. But as impressive as the operations were, they weren't nearly as impressive as the passion with which World Vision's people did their work. The organization was really just a framework within which committed, capable people could live out their calling. I thought about what the people at the nine-couple dinner had told us:

- Find a passion.
- Don't start something new.
- Plug into an existing organization that we believed in.

A passion for Burma, now Myanmar, was already taking shape. And after our trip to Guatemala with World Vision, we found an existing organization that we believed in. After seeing the team members embrace those unwashed, unloved children outside the dump in Guatemala City, it wasn't hard to imagine that their individual acts of love and kindness actually might change the world for millions of people.

Today, World Vision's annual budget is more than two billion dollars. They raise it all every year; there's no endowment. They have almost 50,000 employees from all over the world, and they are active in 100 countries. The complexity of the operation is staggering, and yet the beneficiaries of their work experience a personal touch—a hug, a drink of clean water, an education—not an organization. I always say that World Vision serves as proof to me that there is a God. No human being is good, talented, or smart enough to run an organization like World Vision without divine help.

---

When we got back to the States, Marilyn and I flew to World Vision's headquarters in Los Angeles to meet with Bob Seiple and Cary Paine, who was the organization's vice president at the time. "This all looks very good," I told them. "We're impressed. But tell me. What are you doing in Myanmar?"

"I'm glad you asked," said Bob. The previous year, World Vision had appointed a National Director for Myanmar. He had not yet been in country and the task was daunting. There weren't any non-governmental organizations working in Myanmar at that time, no ambassadors from any free-world country, and the way forward wasn't obvious. I wouldn't have wanted the job of National Director for Myanmar at that time. World Vision's "Myanmar Initial Phase" document painted a pretty stark picture:

> In working in Myanmar, World Vision will be working in a country whose government record on human rights is among the worst in the world and is among the most repressive ... Our work in Myanmar will seek to have a positive influence towards a more just situ-

ation, endeavoring to nurture signs of hope so that transformation can take place.

Talk about incredible timing. It's hard not to believe that God was at work. Marilyn and I just "happened" to be in Burma during the 24 hours that the student demonstrations were gearing up, and so we got a first-hand look at just how badly the people of that country needed help. At the same time, World Vision's fledgling efforts in Myanmar were just getting started but were in dire need of a little more help.

"Would you be willing to consider providing financial support for our work in Myanmar?" Bob asked.

"That's not what I had in mind," I said. Bob blanched a little. "Marilyn and I aren't interested in just providing funds," I explained. "We want to be hands-on partners in forging solutions in that country. " Bob looked visibly relieved. I continued, "And yes, we do want to provide financial support too."

Bob suggested that World Vision arrange for Marilyn and me to join him and Cary Payne on a trip to Myanmar to survey the needs and opportunities that were there.

We made the trip in 1991. We were in country for four days. That might sound like a short trip, but it was four times longer than our previous trip to the country! We met with Christian leaders who told us that they had been praying that someone would come to intervene for the suffering people of Burma, but they were surprised that we had come so soon. If that doesn't make the hairs stand up on the back of your neck, nothing will.

We traveled to rural areas that had absolutely no infrastructure—no roads, just paths, and no electricity, sewage, or running water. On our first trip, we had heard how bad things were and saw a little bit, but we hadn't seen anything like we saw on this trip. We saw the results of the government's disastrous plan to relocate 387,000 of its citizens a year earlier. That fiasco, in a country shunned by the world for its human rights abuses, was a distressingly typical scenario. Given no notice, slum residents, professional people, and middle-class families were loaded into trucks with only what they could carry, driven far from the city and left in four remote "settlements" with no sewers or safe drinking water, and inadequate health care. Meanwhile, the government bulldozed their former homes. The government called it a social intervention to clean up the slums, but it was also a political strategy designed to weaken and control factions that might threaten the government's stronghold.

We visited those settlements to assess whether or not World Vision might provide medical assistance through satellite health clinics. Marilyn and I were astonished to learn that Rangoon had less than 2,500 hospital beds for a population of four million people. Wichita, by contrast, has nearly 2,800 hospital beds for a population of 400,000. In rural areas and especially the new settlements, the healthcare infrastructure was even worse.

On that first trip, we also met with Pei Thain, one of the five generals who ran the country. He was the equivalent of our Secretary of Health and Human Services. The government's deep, long-standing suspicion of outsiders was very obvious. The General played it close to the vest. But Bob and Cary knew what they were doing. They convinced him that World Vision was committed to helping people, not overthrowing the government or proselytizing Buddhists (who make up 85 percent of the country's population). Pei Thain was the reason we could begin working in Burma. He became a friend; we even visited him after he retired.

Over the next year, World Vision produced a Memorandum of Understanding with the Burmese government. Marilyn and I were fully engaged in every step of the process. The gist of the agreement was that World Vision would provide health services in the four townships, which were home to 265,000 residents. World Vision agreed not to proselytize or try to change the government. The last sentence of the agreement—which took a year to negotiate—simply stated that if the Burmese government didn't like what World Vision was doing, World Vision had 24 hours to get out of the country.

We called our plan the "Integrated Health Program for Myanmar." The program would provide health care for children and mothers, safe drinking water, and hygienic facilities. In addition, it would train indigenous healthcare workers to strengthen the delivery of primary healthcare in clinics and hospitals and help the families of handicapped children and leprosy victims provide better care.

Our goals were clear and relatively simple: provide health clinics in the townships, drill tube wells to provide clean water in the Rangoon area, and build fly-proof latrines at schools. The larger goal—the one that had the potential to make the biggest difference—was to prove to the world's NGO community that it was indeed possible to do relief and development work in Myanmar.

One thing I've learned through our work with World Vision is that when you find your passion and pursue it, that passion is contagious. I was visiting Yousef Elakeel, the Saudi friend of mine, shortly after returning from a later survey trip to Burma. We were sitting in the living room of his condominium in San Diego, and I was telling him about what we had seen and were doing. I was in the middle of a sentence when Yousef abruptly stood up from the sofa and disappeared into the next room. He came back with a checkbook.

"Whom should I make this check out to?" he asked. "You? Your company?"

"Excuse me?" I said.

"I like what you're doing," he said. "I want to give money to help."

I thought we were just visiting, just talking. This wasn't a fund-raising effort. But I went with it. "Make it out to World Vision," I said.

He gave me a Euro check for $100,000, designated for the work in Myanmar. Think about that: a Muslim had just given a Christian $100,000 to help Buddhist children half a world away. There are great people everywhere in this world.

Between 1991 and 2008, Marilyn and I made five trips to Myanmar with World Vision. It has been a joy to observe the dramatic success of World Vision's growing platform of holistic community development programs. Highlights include:

- Child sponsorship programs. These are the backbone of World Vision's relief and development efforts—"one child at a time"—in the vast majority of the countries it serves. The Myanmar government was resistant at first; they didn't want to give the impression to the watching world that they relied on outside support to care for their own children. But since the sponsorship program was established, it has supported more than 40,000 children.
- Drop-in centers for at-risk children in both Yangon and Mandalay.
- Clinics focusing on maternity and childcare.
- Fly-proof latrines at schools.
- A microfinance loan program, which has made nearly 40,000 loans totaling $7.7 million.
- The hiring of Myanmaran doctors and hundreds of midwives, whom we were able to provide with ambulances, drugs, uniforms, and bicycles.
- Sixty-five tube wells driven through 40 feet of contaminated water.
- More than 40 Non-Government Organizations (NGOs) now operating in country.

The Integrated Health Program has also set up four HIV-AIDS education stations along Myanmar's border with Thailand. In the border regions, migrant workers, who cross the border for sex, often carry the disease. That region is where it is believed that 90 percent of sex-trade workers are infected.

These centers teach safe sex and distribute condoms. More than 20,000 men have been through the stations.

Another program that has been close to our heart is the Mary Chapman School for the Deaf in Rangoon. The American organization called Heartspring, which treats children with audiological and other disabilities, has had a huge impact on the school. Heartspring also happens to be based in our hometown of Wichita, Kansas. In 1995, four audiologists travelled to Rangoon with testing equipment and hearing aids that our foundation was privileged to provide. A couple of hundred kids could hear for the first time after two weeks of hard work by these dedicated women. On our next trip to Burma, we went to the Mary Chapman School. When we arrived, the children, when told that we had supplied the hearing aids, all gathered and with sign language said, "I love you." Tears were flowing down both of our cheeks.

---

One day, Marilyn and I were shocked to receive a personal letter from Colonel Than Zin, Myanmar's Deputy Minister of Health. It read, "I assure that the work and progress of your organization can run effectively and efficiently in the four townships and more. We also like to extend your action a few more townships in coming years." Reflecting on the suspicion with which the military junta eyed us during that first meeting, we couldn't believe that World Vision was being invited to expand their efforts. World Vision has now expanded into more than 25 ADPs.

It had been a long road. In the early days, the problem wasn't a lack of receptivity. The government was actually moderately receptive. The problem was more that it was inexperienced at dealing with NGOs or outsiders of any sort. There were no established protocols for NGOs working in Burma. It was unclear, for instance, if World Vision was supposed to report to the military, the President, or the Ministry of Health.

Expatriate World Vision project managers who wished to travel to project offices first had to obtain permission from a Burmese government agency. Sometimes permission was granted, but sometimes it wasn't, and the reasons why were never clear. Two of World Vision's project offices were in states where expatriates were not allowed to travel. Once, it took World Vision nine months to transfer the registration of four vehicles. One World Vision staffer was sentenced to two years in prison for allowing someone to stay overnight in his house without first asking permission.

While the work has been going forward in Burma, World Vision has worked hard to apply pressure on our Congress to adopt more positive approaches to Burma, rather than ongoing sanctions, diplomatic neglect, and a near total absence of investment, which have been characteristic of our relationship (or lack thereof) with Burma. But Burma doesn't figure into America's strategic interests, so it doesn't warrant serious attention from our government. Our neglect has been part of the reason that NGOs had been historically deterred from getting involved in a country that needs them.

The goal of any philanthropist is for the projects one supports to take root, to take on a life of their own. That is what has happened in Myanmar. In the early days, World Vision relied on the DeBoer Family Foundation to support all (or nearly all) the work in Burma. Today, many countries are involved in the financial support of World Vision's efforts in country. Now our foundation supports special projects, including the drop-in centers in Rangoon and Mandalay. Meanwhile, World Vision's Burma operations have grown substantially. The four original health clinics now serve 10,000 patients each month. World Vision has about 700 employees in Burma, most of them locals, and about 1,500 volunteers. The annual budget of World Vision Myanmar is $13 million, with funds coming from Australia, the United Kingdom, Taiwan, Japan, Germany, France, New Zealand, Korea, Malaysia, Singapore, and Spain.

Since our first trip, more than three million people have directly benefited from World Vision's work.

One of my favorite things about World Vision's work is that they paved the way for other NGOs. There were no NGOs in Myanmar when we first visited. Now there are more than 40. World Vision has helped show governments, NGOs, and other donors throughout the world that people really can make a difference in the world, one child at a time. Seeds of help (and hope) can grow almost anywhere in the world.

---

There's a story in the Bible where Jesus sits in the synagogue and watches the people come through and put their offerings in the treasury. The rich people come through, write their big checks, and throw their sacks of gold coin in the bucket and Jesus yawns. But then, a little old lady shuffles up to the front and, a little embarrassed, tosses two tiny coins in the treasury that together add up to no more than a penny. And Jesus sits up and takes notice. He says, "Truly I say to you, this poor widow put in more than all the contributors to the treasury; for they all put in out of their surplus, but she, out of her poverty, put in all she owned, all she had to live on."

Pursuing our calling in Burma has been one of the most rewarding things that Marilyn and I have ever done. But even talking about it embarrasses me; it embarrasses me to think that anybody might think we're trying to claim some kind of credit, gather laurels, or sing our own praises. Let me say right here that our giving has never affected our lifestyle. It is somewhat embarrassing to know that we've never given to the point that we have ever made a sacrifice that really hurt. In other words, I can say—hopefully without the least bit of false humility—that there is nothing heroic about our philanthropic effort.

I'll tell you who my hero is. My hero is the middle-class father who says, "Sorry, kids. We aren't going out to eat this month because we've got to fulfill our pledge to the church." My hero is the single mom who shares her already crowded home with a friend who has nowhere else to stay.

That's genuine philanthropy. That's my hero.

# A Wife's Perspective

In the '50s, Jack started putting $100 in my account every Friday for household expenses and anything I might choose to purchase. Back then, that was a lot of money. I have always been a frugal person, and I still am today. I clip coupons and I shop the sales. When Jack first started developing subdivisions, his business expenses increased much more than he anticipated, and I wondered if I would get the $100 every Friday. But I always did. However, Jack and I didn't talk about it. It has just been within the last five years that he has opened up and shared his businesses. Part of this was my own doing. I do not relate to numbers. Part of it was just how it was done in those days. We each had our roles to play. Jack took care of business and I took care of the home.

"Risk Only Money." The title of this book implies the presence of other important factors in your life— your integrity, your friendships, and your family. There are many business people who have racked up economic success but have lost everything else. You are not likely to make the leap from success to significance without your integrity, friends, or family. Of all the lessons offered in the book, this is perhaps the most crucial.

Most people have heard the saying, "Behind every great man stands a woman." I think a better way of describing my relationship with Jack is this: "*Beside* every great man stands a woman." My idea was not to "serve him" in the sense that I would be subservient, responding to his every whim. Instead, I was there at his side making it easy for him to come home. He didn't need another mom, and he didn't need more stress when he walked through the door. To the modern reader, this might give the impression that I was dependent on Jack or that he considered his occupation more important than mine. It shouldn't.

The truth is, I have always been very independent. I began working at age 16 and continued until I had children. At college, I participated in sorority rush, but when I didn't get the bid from the sorority I wanted, I stayed an independent. I became a "traditional housewife" and mother because it was what I wanted.

The women's liberation movement held no appeal for me. I was already living the life of my choice, and I never considered my role to be any less important than Jack's. Nobody succeeds alone. As Jack has said, "A great business partnership needs both an entrepreneur and a manager." The same idea can apply to a marriage partnership. He was the family entrepreneur. I was the family manager.

I was never involved in the details of Jack's business. At the time, I did not know he had thousands of creditors. I simply knew him—his character, integrity, and competence. I never doubted Jack's ability. I never pressured him. When I did realize that things at work were not going as he had hoped and planned—particularly when he spent those two days in bed worrying about how he would repay his creditors—I never called Jack a failure. For his part, Jack was home for dinner with his family every night when he wasn't traveling on business. I was by Jack's side through the ups and downs of business. His success was my success. Yes, Jack was gone a lot of the time during the week, and often I wished he was at home more. But even after he

*(continued)*

had achieved the financial success that he discusses in this book, well after we had plenty of money for our own use, I told him that I wanted him to keep working in his business to make money that we could give to others.

After the trip around the world in 1988, I felt I was beginning to see the reason that we had been blessed with health, energy, and resources. It was at that point that we started getting serious about giving back, largely through World Vision in Burma. Through our charity work, our marriage partnership has grown sweeter and stronger. It has been the most rewarding, adventurous time of our lives, made possible in part by all of the years spent striving together. Significance is best when it is shared, when you haven't given up those things that are most important in life. It's true what Jack says: Risk only money.

*—Marilyn DeBoer*

# 12

# From Success to Significance: Some Principles for Philanthropy

S o, what is significance? My definition is what you do in your life to make a positive difference in the lives of others. Success, when you come down to it, isn't really success unless it serves a purpose much larger than self. In other words, success is nothing compared to significance. If we're willing to plan for success and work systematically for it, shouldn't we do the same for significance? Marilyn and I slowly began to make the transition to sharing with others, but as the success became more positive, significance began to play a much more important role in our lives.

In my career, I have found that the only way to sustain success is to do work that you're passionate about—where your interests, talents, and disposition are all engaged. For example, I've written at length about the importance of entrepreneurs being entrepreneurs and managers being managers. When we try to be someone at the office that's different from who we are inside, it's not going to work out well—not for long, anyway.

For better or worse, my work has always been an extension of me. In the days of runaway me, my business was marked by runaway ego. As my outlook on life changed in the '70s, my companies changed accordingly.

After our first visit to Burma, we realized that God had a different plan for us that reached far beyond the construction and lodging business. The passion Marilyn and I developed for Burma—a place where the world's great need was so obvious as to be unmistakable—was itself a vocation. It was almost like we had no choice but to work on making a difference. We realized that we were not just obligated to philanthropy as good civic leaders. We felt *called* to philanthropy.

Just as I would have never gone about my career in a willy-nilly fashion, Marilyn and I knew we had to be proactive in the way we went about the vocation of philanthropy and plan carefully. Otherwise, we would end up responding to the squeakiest wheel to come through the office asking for money. And that would have been a recipe for ineffectiveness—not to mention bitterness. I've seen a lot of well-meaning people sour on their philanthropic efforts because they were *reacting* and *responding* to requests and ended up giving their hard-earned money and valuable time to efforts that, although noble, did not have the basics of making a difference and simply adding money was not the solution.

As I look back on my career, I've never done well when I've gone against my own instincts or was living by someone else's values or judgment. When I pursued my career to impress my mother, I ended up losing my bearings, pursuing ego, and crashing badly. I didn't last long when I tried to go along with partners or investors who were doing things just to pad the balance sheet or put up big numbers. Every time I tried to collaborate with someone who had different objectives than I did (even if it was not a moral difference, but simply a different business approach), it went bad before long. There were times I tried to convince myself that the person I was dealing with was on the up and up when I really suspected they were shady. Those times turned sour too.

Well, in our "significance stage," Marilyn and I realized that our philanthropy should be just as focused, thought-out, and demanding as my business dealings had been. After Odyssey 88, we realized it was time to get serious about giving back. That meant having a plan. We came up with a few principles that have guided all the giving we have done since the night we invited the nine couples to our post-travel dinner. I offer them here not as a blueprint for how everybody ought to give, but as an example of how we arrived at a plan.

This chapter is a long one. But I hope you'll stay with me. You don't want to get stuck at success. You want to enjoy the fruits of living a life of significance.

## 1. Giving is personal.

Marilyn and I knew that our plan had to be a personalized plan. We knew about the great philanthropy practiced by such giants as Rockefeller and Carnegie, and later the Buffet's and Gates' of the world. Our philanthropy would need to represent the hopes and vision of Jack and Marilyn DeBoer: sweethearts from Kalamazoo, Michigan, parents of two and grandparents of three, longtime citizens of Wichita, Kansas, with all of our various avocations. Our philanthropy needed to reflect our faith and values. It needed to reflect loyalty and include our friends. And it needed to reflect a guy who has tried hard to conduct business at the highest levels—often successfully but not always—and whose main confidante is still the girl he met in high school. It would be an outgrowth of the couple who are deeply saddened when they see people sleeping on the streets, living out of shopping carts, or making decisions based on just a few dollars.

I would never tell anyone how he ought to give—even if I thought I was qualified to do so. I would only say that your giving should be guided by a plan that reflects the values that guide your life. Your passions are different from ours. It would be a pretty dull world if they weren't. Our son and daughter are involved in different causes than we are. Why? The things they care most deeply about are different from the things we care most deeply about. If helping an inner-city school in Chicago or Colorado is what fulfills their passion for others and their values—well, we can live with that! In fact we whole-heartedly support it.

## 2. Philanthropy is a free market.

I'm convinced that our differing passions is one of the main ways that God gets his work done on this complex planet of ours. Passion meets need: I call it the philanthropy free market. In the free market of business, the entrepreneur makes a living by finding a need and filling it. Whenever there is an untapped business opportunity, money flows to that void. The free market ensures that some entrepreneur will try to tap that opportunity. It's the same with philanthropy. Except that I don't really think it's a vague free market; it's God calling people like Marilyn and me in directions that grow out of their particular makeups. So in the philanthropy free market, each of us finds a need that lines up with our passions and fills it, not for our own profit, but for the good of people who are in need.

## 3. Family foundations add value for hands-on donors.

We're often asked why we chose to create our own foundation. That's an excellent question, especially in light of the community foundations like The Wichita Foundation, which serves

Marilyn's and my hometown so well. Community foundations serve donors of all giving levels in many ways:

- Informing donors about varied deserving local causes.
- Training donors with insights into charitable giving.
- Convening groups of donors to address current community needs.
- Connecting donors who have common interests.
- Advising charities about management issues.
- Advocating for the nonprofit sector before city and state officials.
- Informing donors about city, state, and national legal and tax developments.
- Disbursing donors' gifts at specified times and for specified causes.
- Providing donors with accounting and recordkeeping services, including receipts and reports.
- Allowing timing of gifts for tax purposes.

For years, I've viewed The Wichita Foundation as a powerful partner in making Wichita a better place. More personally, it has also been a nice resource to my family foundation, as we've compared notes and shared information on local causes.

We did choose to create our own family foundation, though—a decision that suits us better each year. We started a family foundation for personal, family, and financial reasons of our own—reasons that won't apply to everyone. Let me explain why a family foundation was the best solution for Marilyn and me.

In the past, we've used our foundation as a conduit, on a money-in/money-out basis. The foundation has always given money out soon after it was received. That will change in the future, though, because as a centerpiece of our estate plans, the foundation will grow considerably. Having our own family foundation allows for greater flexibility and control as we look toward the next generation.

Marilyn and I have a variety of giving interests, from Wichita to other U.S. causes to Burma. We place a high value on doing research in all of the areas where we get philanthropically involved. Our foundation needs to continually gather information on a wide array of local, national, and international issues and organizations. Sometimes the research we need is complex intelligence from the world's top scholars, politicians, and leading practitioners. At other times, it's merely a matter of meeting charities' leaders and "kicking the tires" on the organization.

This is a major reason why having our own foundation, and a professional to run it, is invaluable. The fulltime president of our foundation spends all of his time on our projects: researching the charities we support and the countries and regions we serve; interacting with the charities' leaders, whether helping or holding them accountable; doing site visits to charities; forging collaborations with other foundations and givers; networking with influencers of all sorts; coordinating the administrative details of our foundation; and more. I admit that this is a significant expenditure, but Marilyn and I believe that it's one of the most important investments we can make. We feel that evaluating where our foundation resources are deployed is more difficult than making decisions to make the best returns in business. No, let me restate that: The money we pay our president is a great investment because he is the positive multiplier in every one of our granting relationships. I often say to friends that to me, making money was easier than giving it away effectively.

Our foundation's president is Fritz Kling. His background perfectly equips him to research and consult. He ran a university fundraising shop over one decade, and ran a foundation shop for another, so he has been on both sides of the giving table. He has overseen grants of millions of dollars and has run start-up charities with tiny budgets. He also practiced law. In sum, a strong Christian, he knows how to deal with facts, organizations, and leaders.

One of the great things about our family foundation is not only that we're able to give money to charities, but also to help them become stronger in the process. This is our foundation's consulting role, and we love it when Fritz can help charities in this way. This is a role our board values highly, and I've described it below in the "Money is not the only currency" section.

## 4. Put dollars where dollars are scarce.

Coming to understand the philanthropy free market was liberating for me because it allowed me to express myself in giving money just as I'd done in making money. In business, I'd sought out new markets and didn't need a road map. If no one had done it before, all the better.

In philanthropy, when we experienced Burma and its desperate plight, Marilyn and I were deeply intrigued. We're very relational, and when we got to know the people, we were persuaded that Burma would have a special role in our lives. And then, when we saw that so few other people, countries, or agencies in the world seemed to give much thought to Burma, we were hooked. Today's statistics bear that out: In 2007, overseas assistance to Burma totaled $4.08 per person. To put that in perspective, Laos received $58 per person, Sudan $58, and Zimbabwe $41. Here was a market with huge needs (and opportunities for good) and little outside investment. It had our name written all over it.

You may approach things differently, and I thank God for that. There are many other needs, many of which will require huge concentrations of generous people who want to give where others are also giving. It's a good thing that there are more of those kinds of people, because that way I don't have to feel guilty about how I feel called to give! At my age, after all I've seen, it's the farthest thing from my heart and mind to judge others negatively for how they answer their philanthropic calling. So, whether you like to cluster with other donors or if, like Marilyn and me, you choose to spread out with different causes, just figure out how you're wired and give in that way. Marilyn and I love that we are committed to Burma while our neighbors and colleagues may be committed to the local homeless shelter or to their church or synagogue. To us, Burma seemed an obvious choice in part because it hasn't been an obvious choice for others.

Almost by definition, giving money where money is scarce has meant that most of our philanthropic dollars end up overseas. We try to be generous in our hometown of Wichita, but we also know that there are many people in Wichita who are using their money to meet needs there. We understand the principle that charity begins at home. But for us, the desire to put dollars where dollars are scarce usually trumps the desire to give closer to home.

As a corollary to this principle, dollars tend to go farther where dollars are scarce. In Burma, the per capita income in 2008 was $1,200. So how much good will $1,000 do in a Burmese village as compared to Wichita, where the per capita income is more than $20,000? That's pretty easy math.

## 5. Focus.

Every day, the DeBoer Foundation receives several requests from charities and causes that are perfectly deserving of our help (not to mention a few that aren't deserving!). Any philanthropist who wishes to diversify his giving portfolio has ample opportunity. And many philanthropists do choose to diversify across many causes or countries. Instead of diversifying, Marilyn and I have chosen to focus. In the beginning, our investment in Burma was sustaining almost all of the efforts that we had chosen; but as the years passed, others came to help Burma, so we slowed our efforts there and searched for other places to invest. The foundation worked with World Vision to search for another Burma, but as time passed, it became clear to us that our heart was in Burma. In 20 years, the population grew from 45 million to more than 60 million and conditions were not improving. Fritz is now deeply involved in an assessment of Burma to determine what we can do to plant more seeds in the country.

If you choose to diversify, good for you. The important thing is that you *choose* to diversify instead of accidentally diversifying because you find it hard to turn down a good sales pitch. Marilyn and I have heard dozens of brilliant sales pitches by people who are doing great work—passionate, good people who we knew would make excellent use of whatever money we might give them. The vast majority of the time, we have wished those people well and sent them away not quite empty handed, but with only a small gift.

## 6. Ego-holics and anonymity.

Programs or buildings with our name on them are non-starters. We're not interested. Remember, I'm a recovering ego-holic, and stuff named for me would only serve to get my ego back in the equation. I learned long ago to avoid this kind of involvement, so now we most often give anonymously.

What, you might ask, about Marilyn? Would *she* like to see a DeBoer Hall or a Jack and Marilyn DeBoer Health Clinic? Like me, she doesn't care about seeing her name in public. You see, she's never had an ego problem. Never, that is, except one named Jack!

## 7. Money isn't the only kind of currency— or even the most important.

Giving, for us, isn't just about giving money. We want to be as involved as possible in the larger causes we've chosen. It's not a question of maintaining control over our "investment" or of meddling in the charity's affairs. I can assure you, at 80 years old I'm not looking for more people to manage, projects to run, or budgets to meet. It's more about getting totally behind something. Come on, let's be honest with each other: Many charities with great missions and heart lack the business skills that are important for sustainability. And charities are in business too.

Marilyn and I love to take opportunities for non-financial giving. We host events in Wichita, and our foundation often lends its expertise—hard-earned knowledge from years of experience—to help charities at pivotal times.

Not too long ago, we learned of a tiny charity that was doing some good work, but it was on the rocks. It had financial, personnel, and leadership problems. A promising young man led the charity, but the organization was broke and dysfunctional. They asked us for money. We liked what their organization was doing, but we were sure that money would not solve their crisis. A new board, empowered leadership, a shored-up facility, more volunteers, and, of course, money ... now *that* might give them a chance! But we realized that a substantial financial gift would just be a waste if that was all we gave them. That might keep the doors open for a few more months, but that's all it would do.

So we gave them non-financial gifts before we gave them a financial gift. We sent Fritz over to consult with them and walk them through problem solving. First of all, we gave them up-front money to keep the doors open. For several months, its top leaders were working without pay (with the young Executive Director taking unemployment). In addition, we offered to match whatever grants they could raise from other donors. We like to make challenge grants to underperforming grantees, but we recognized that such a grant to this organization would be useless because they only had $2,000 and would have to close their doors before they could raise much money.

The Executive Director was encouraged by our money and offer of more, so he was eager for our conditions. We told him that, in order to meet our challenge grant, he would have to: 1) make a six-month plan for the charity's recovery, and make regular phone calls and emails with Fritz to discuss his progress; 2) recruit a new, strong Board; and, 3) recruit substantially more volunteers. We very clearly told them that they could accept our up-front money and leave it at that if they had other plans or better offers. We noted that their Board had overseen contraction of the charity from a budget of around $150,000 to $2,000 in just three years, and that they clearly needed a drastic change.

Apart from Fritz's experience, having a fresh set of eyes look at a problem is always a big help. We pour lots of time and effort into undergirding the nonprofit community because we believe that our foundation's greatest assets are not just money.

## 8. Identify good leaders and back them.

Fritz saw great potential in the Executive Director, and saw that he was the organization's best (and perhaps only) hope for the future. What that charity needed was not an infusion of funds. It needed something much more sustainable: strengthened leadership. That need was especially acute since the new leader was only 25 years old.

The experience with the struggling charity ended wonderfully. Just six months later, Marilyn, Fritz and I met with the Executive Director in my company's conference room. What a great joy for Marilyn and me! He recounted the period in which he had poured himself selflessly and tirelessly into reviving the charity, and their uncommitted checking account had gone from $0 to $22,000. He had requested and received gifts from individuals and also local corporations and foundations. In addition, he had recruited an expanded and much-strengthened Board. And there were also more volunteers. It was now able to continue with its mission to help young men and women in a depressed section of Wichita.

If our foundation had only given the up-front money, the organization would not have improved as much as it did.

What gave us great confidence was that we invested in a person who would guide them for the coming years. We thought he had potential. When we held out some challenges and opportunities to him, he responded impressively. That's the kind of sharp leader we want to work with when we make our grants.

## 9. Bring others along for the ride.

Like all of these philanthropic principles, this one is a reflection of Marilyn's and my approach to life. Almost anything we like doing, we enjoy more with friends along for the ride. I'm a cheerleader, and I've always been one: on the shop floor, in meetings with Wall Street investors, on Wichita civic projects, and also with our philanthropic causes. Some call it shameless, the way I'm always pitching Burma and World Vision in my conversations and speeches, and even our Christmas letters. All I know is that, over the past decade, dozens of Marilyn's and my friends have given hundreds of thousands of dollars to help starving, desperate, and dying children in a country on the other side of the world. Keep in mind that not once did I ask anyone for money. Bob Seiple wondered one day how much money we could raise if I were to ask. I've already told the story of my Saudi friend who gave a $100,000 check to World Vision after hearing me speak of my passion for Burma. As a result of my loud mouthing and their generosity, all of us—the donors, the Burmese, and Marilyn and I—are living lives of more significance.

## 10. Fix leaky roofs.

I may have given the impression that we never give to hometown causes. It's true that the bulk of our giving ends up in Burma, but we do give to causes in Wichita. We have a slightly different philosophy for domestic giving. Much of the Burma work we're involved in is long-term, strategic, and infrastructure-related. We've helped drill tube wells and install fly-proof latrines. In a world without infrastructure, helping one child at a time starts with strategizing and laying groundwork. In Wichita, our emphasis is on charities that help children and down-and-out men and women in the immediate term.

Many donors and foundations give strategically for long-term impact, and that's a good thing, but what really impacts us are the people sleeping under overpasses or single moms who can't pay for electricity or transportation to emergency rooms. This really hit home a few years ago when Wichita's social service community was plunged into the depths of a perfect storm. First, our area was slammed by massive layoffs in the aerospace industry, namely at Cessna and Hawker Beech. That left a lot of families with involuntarily idle breadwinners, unable to pay for baby formula, utilities, blankets, car repairs, or Christmas gifts. Second, giving was beginning a several-year slide, as donors were feeling the need to pinch dollars more than in previous years. And finally, since the demand for social services was at an all-time high, the local charities that had seen their revenues dwindle had to do much more with a lot less. Fortunately, many of the needy were able to continue their productive lives and only needed short-term assistance to get them through a tough time. I know what it's like to feel that you're on the brink of ruin and how much of a difference it makes to know that somebody is on your side.

That December, a local homeless shelter approached us with a need. We learned that they had a leaky roof, which was causing moisture, mildew, and drafts for the overflow crowd of men sleeping on cots and pads on the floor below. It occurred to us that this was *exactly* the kind of local need we wanted to support. We helped them with their roof, and ever since, we've talked about "Leaky Roof gifts"—those gifts that help people with immediate physical needs, today.

I may be stating the obvious here, but we're not opposed to long-term, strategic, capital-focused giving. We're glad for the Gates Foundation with their investments in studies and policy research. It's a good thing there are others who invest in computer upgrades, conferences, and marketing plans. That's the philanthropy free market at work. Those people's passions align with different needs than ours do. In the case of Burma, we need to invest money that will lay the groundwork for continued growth, but in Wichita, it is the short-term leaky roof that gets our attention.

## 11. Commit to loyalty and teamwork.

Loyalty has been important to Marilyn and me throughout our lives. We've maintained lifelong friendships with people from Michigan, Wichita neighbors, and workers from my different companies. We like to develop lasting relationships, and have also done so in our charitable involvements. For example, the first two World Vision officials whom we met 20 years ago, Drs. Cary Paine and Bob Seiple, became lifelong friends and are now members of the DeBoer Family Foundation's Board.

When we get involved with charities, it is always with the possibility and hope to develop relationships that will be long lasting. We know that, in order to help places from Wichita to Burma, we need to empower and support the people who are doing the job. Once we find good organizations and people to support, we hope to stay loyally behind them. That is why we have great regard and fondness for the World Vision staff, visiting with them in Wichita, Washington, DC, New York, Seattle, and Burma.

This is not the way all donors do their giving. Many donors choose to spread their money around, and to move from one grantee to another. And, I certainly see the wisdom in that, because it keeps grantees from taking a donor for granted and organizations from becoming dependent upon an individual donor. But, as I noted earlier, all donors must find ways to give that reflect and fit within their own lives. For us, that means sticking with the charities that are doing a great job.

## 12. Use your brain.

One of the unique aspects of the charity world is that it is so heart-driven. Because the causes involved are so important and Earth-breaking—whether they be saving souls, feeding hungry mouths, clothing the naked, building homes, saving the Earth, saving whales, hiring veterans, or many other causes—the stakes and the passions are high. The downside, in my opinion, is that the charitable world is filled with leaders who function completely from the heart and leave the head out of it. That's not to say that they're not bright, but they don't like to think organizationally. We think that the deepest needs of society can be best served by a healthy combination of social service depth and compassion and business efficiency and analysis. That is the approach we try to bring.

At our foundation, we use our brains by doing our homework. We invest huge amounts of time and energy in meeting with leaders of different charities, with subject matter experts from around the world, and by researching our areas of giving. It is very easy to give money away poorly. I don't like doing anything poorly.

Now, I know that the charitable or social service worlds don't run like clockwork, like businesses sometimes do. Charities deal with a lack of funds, poor equipment and facilities, underpaid staff, overwhelming needs, throbbing heart-driven people, and constant emergencies beyond their control. I concluded long ago that, if a person wants to operate in a predictable, sane, controllable environment, they had better stay away from the social services—to say nothing of Burma! So we try to realize that we are entering a parallel universe when we deal with charities, even though we expect the best out of them. I admit that it can be a hard balance to strike, but I'm a lot better at it at 80 than I was at 60. Now, I know that significance looks very different from success.

### 13. Encourage those on the front lines.

A theme throughout our giving is that it is not about us, but about the organization and cause we're supporting. Whether charitable funding comes from a hotel developer, an information technology entrepreneur, or an investment banker doesn't matter; what matters is that the Wichita homeless shelter or Burma center for street children can stay afloat to serve the needy. After Marilyn and I and our foundation are gone, I know others will rise up to meet those needs.

The key players, then, are the people who run the charities. They're the stars. If they're not good, encouraged, or motivated, or if the organization is not solvent, then Jack and Marilyn DeBoer are helpless to meet those needs. We count on those people to be great at what they do. And when we find great organizations run by great people, we like to stay loyal to them. And we like to stay out of their way. We really just want to let the experts do their work. There may be areas where Fritz or we can help from time to time, for instance in issues of strategic planning, marketing, or fundraising. But, for the most part, the amazing folks at Wichita's Union Rescue Mission (and Center of Hope, Pregnancy Crisis Center, Salvation Army, Via Christi, and all the other charities we support) know more about their field than Marilyn, Fritz, and I combined will ever know.

And there's one other aspect of this principle. Once we find a great charity that has strong leadership, we like to help it with its general operating needs. Lots of donors like to give to special or new projects, and I understand that. I think their approach is to be catalysts for new progress and developments, and to expect the charity's base of general supporters to cover overhead. But a charity can get strung out, always looking for the next budget dollar. I don't like for my companies to exist under that kind of pressure, and don't wish that for the charities I most admire. So Marilyn and I prefer to give money today, to be used now, and not for new projects.

That reminds me of my role in the philanthropic equation. I'm like the guy in the steam engine who shovels coal into the fire. I didn't build the train. I'm not the destination. I'm not even driving the rig. I'm just the guy with the shovel, whose calling is to help fuel the machine.

### 14. We're not an ATM.

We are not the saviors of any charities. No charity will thrive because of Jack and Marilyn DeBoer; if it thrives, it will be because of the vision, work, and sacrifice of an army of other folks.

Further, we can give hundreds of thousands or millions of dollars to charity, but it won't thrive unless that money is used wisely. Fritz told me that when he worked at the University of Richmond, they used to say, "No university ever became great because of big money. But no university ever became great without lots of money."

At the same time, we take comfort in knowing that no charity will fail *for lack of* our money. If a charity fails, it will be because of actions done—or not done—over years, not because of our decision whether to support it. So guilt trips don't work on us. I'm just not that important in the philanthropic scheme of things.

But a big role we can play is for the foundation, and for Fritz specifically, to mentor, encourage, and challenge leaders. An example of this is our desire to keep charities honest and to exhibit "tough love." One year, Fritz told me that one of his favorite charities didn't come prepared to the year-end meeting; no statistics about what they'd accomplished, reports on how past money had been used, forecasts for the next year, or trends analysis in its field. It'd received grants from us, several years in a row, and this year they seemed to "phone it in."

It seemed the charity had begun to view our foundation as an ATM: You show up and we spit out money. That was disappointing, both because it didn't demonstrate much respect for us as supporters, and also because it didn't reflect how the organization had grown and improved over the year. We never want to enable a stagnating, sloppy charity because charities, like businesses, need to be constantly improving. We're pretty easy to please. In fact, that is not even important, but if a charity doesn't put forth a modicum of effort, then it's getting too casual with something that is very serious to us—giving away our money. We decided to give that particular charity a nominal gift, much less than the previous few years. We hope to support them more in the future and that they don't take our, or any gift, for granted. That's no way to run a charity.

## 15. Visit and listen.

There is no substitute for visiting charities in the field. The brochures never give nearly as good a feel for a charity as does a sit-down with the leader at the community center or homeless shelter.

I love to hear the stories of the charitable leaders Marilyn and I have met. For my money, they are every bit as interesting as the stories I hear at CEO gatherings ... if not more. These charity heads are bright, their interests have taken them to out-of-the-way places, their "constituencies" are never boring, and they are in their line of work because they love people. I find them fascinating.

Also, I'm always fascinated by the actual "stuff" of their jobs: What causes poverty? Why is homelessness more or less severe in one city? How does education correlate to ethnicity? What are the key factors causing abuse? Why is murder up some years and down others? What does it take to turn around a city school? Are microenterprise programs best run by a large nonprofit or a small community-based group? And I've always found that one of the very best ways to show respect and honor for charity workers is to truly value and be interested in what they do.

So, if you like to hear interesting stories about people and society, begin to hang out with charity workers. This is also a great way to get better at giving, by familiarizing yourself with the lay of the land and gauging where your money is most needed and can best be used.

Remember that giving to charity is much more than money. I often feel that it is easy to write the check but hard to do the work everyday. People who run the charities of the world are God's special people called to a life of serving others. Yes, you are our heroes.

# Epilogue

# Anyway

There is a poem that has meant a great deal to me as I have made the slow transition from success to significance. This poem is written on the wall in Mother Teresa's orphanage in Calcutta, India. Based on a piece originally written by Dr. Kent M. Keith in 1968, this poem puts into perspective every effort to do the right thing:

> People are often unreasonable, irrational, and self-centered.
> Forgive them anyway.
> If you are kind, people may accuse you of selfish, ulterior motives.
> Be kind anyway.
> If you are successful, you will win some unfaithful friends and some genuine enemies.
> Succeed anyway.

If you are honest and sincere people may deceive you.

Be honest and sincere anyway.

What you spend years creating, others could destroy overnight.

Create anyway.

If you find serenity and happiness, some may be jealous.

Be happy anyway.

The good you do today will often be forgotten.

Do good anyway.

Give the best you have, and it will never be enough.

Give your best anyway.

In the final analysis, it is between you and God.

It was never between you and them anyway.

Over the course of my career, I put a lot of money at risk. I lost a lot of money, and I gained a lot of money. But it was only money. It was made for risking, losing, and gaining back. That's what business is about. In a very real sense, that's the only thing business is about.

Repeatedly, I've seen people ruin their lives because they think business is about something other than money. I could have easily been one of those people. But I should make something clear. When I say that *business* is only about money, I'm not saying that *life* is only about money. I'm saying the opposite: Life is about *far* more than money or business. With age and wisdom, I've learned to put money and business in their places. Money is a tool that can be used to help extract real meaning out of life. As tools go, it's pretty important. But still, it's only a tool, and a tool is only significant insofar as it helps us accomplish some other task. In other words, getting a hammer, nails, and lumber is no big deal. Using a hammer, nails, and lumber to build a house—that's an accomplishment.

My life has been three journeys punctuated by two "awaken-ings." For 40 years, I was on a journey of striving for self and ego. My first big awakening came in the 1970s when my business world crashed around me. That was the moment in my life when I first realized how foolish it was to use my business as a means of pursuing my ego. When my world came crash-ing down, when I cowered in my bed trying to hide from the harsh reality of thousands of creditors, I reached the end of my striving stage. I had an "aha" moment, a born-again experience, and I made some major changes for the better. But I still wasn't where I needed to be. The next stage was what I call my success stage because I was gaining wisdom—it was the point where my experiences and knowledge turned into insights and per-spective. It was our trip around the world—and specifically our visit to Burma—that made me realize that finding real meaning in life was going to depend on my commitment to the good of other people. That stage—it's the one Marilyn and I are in now—I call significance.

I'm not trying to be holier-than-thou. In fact, I feel I was a late bloomer. It took me a long time and I resisted God in get-ting to my significance stage. But, boy, am I glad I've gotten there. Without it, I think that I'd be a stunted person: fully-grown, with lots of toys and friends and accolades, but sadly underdeveloped in the most important ways.

We can't be who we were made to be unless we give our resources and ourselves to other people. I've always been about ROI—return on investment. In my early years, the return I was ultimately looking for was an increase in what others thought of me. All my moneymaking efforts were invested in growing the Jack P. DeBoer image. In the early 1970s, I learned that it was a sucker's deal. It just didn't work. I had invested all this energy and money in so many of the wrong things, and then I realized that I didn't like myself. There was no return on that investment.

In the following years, I had a better sense of what money, time, and resources are for. I enjoyed some real business success, unlike the house of cards that I had built through the '60s. But there was still something missing.

We're all looking for happiness and fulfillment. Whatever else we're investing in, we're always investing in those things, one way or another. In 1988, I discovered that when it comes to happiness and fulfillment, the most efficient and effective use of my energy and resources was giving to others. That's what I mean when I say there's nothing holier-than-thou about my approach to giving. Marilyn and I give because we get genuine satisfaction from our giving. Burma has done more for us than we did for Burma.

It's almost like a developmental stage. Just as a baby learns to crawl, walk, and then run, we understand more and more about ourselves and God's world we live in. We reach a stage where getting and spending isn't enough; we need to give.

Just this morning, I met with a young man who runs a small and struggling Wichita charity. I saw in him levels of ambition that reminded me of myself at that age ... except that he's already practicing serving others and actively pursuing significance. For sure, he'll need to master his own career skills, like any young man, and I hope he becomes great at the day-in, day-out skills of his chosen profession. But I am pretty certain that he'll skip the foolishness I got mired in, like self-feeding, mindless competitiveness, and obliviousness to the most important things in life. He's already getting a handle on those things. He makes less today than I made at his age—and that was 60 years ago—but in other ways, he's so much further along than I was.

That's why God gave Marilyn and me Burma, to move from success to significance. Some people don't have to go to the other side world to wake up to what's important. But we did.

Marilyn has often said, "I want to live my life as if I am the only Bible other people will ever read." Marilyn has certainly lived her life that way, and it is an admirable goal that I haven't always lived up to. There are many things I wish I had done differently, but I hope as you have read about my life and its lessons that you have found some truths that will help you do things differently and better. I have written this book in hopes that you might better enjoy a wonderful life and make it to the significance stage more easily (and sooner!) than I did. I hope you have found a few lessons that will make your life even happier and more fulfilling. Thanks for taking this journey with me.

God bless.